Psychosomatic
CONCEPTS

COMMENTARY

Dr. Grinker's *Psychosomatic Concepts* is the book universally credited with having brought scientific order into this complicated field. Part of this task had to be destructive of the dreams of the pioneers led by Franz Alexander; this book had to record the failure of Alexander's "specificity" theory that each of seven diseases were aroused by unexpressible specific emotions. But Dr. Grinker's main task was to develop an alternative theory and a blueprint for action, and it is this theory and blueprint which has guided his work and that of many others during the past twenty years. This book remains indispensable to anyone interested in psychosomatic medicine.

PSYCHOSOMATIC CONCEPTS

By Roy R. Grinker, M.D.

Revised Edition

New York • Jason Aronson • London

AT LAST FOR

M.B.G.

WHO WAS ALWAYS FIRST

Contents

Preface

There has been little progress in the field of psychosomatic medicine in the last two decades. In fact in a recent editorial entitled "What's the Payoff in Hypertensive Research" *(Psychosomatic Medicine* 35:1-3, 1973) A. M. Ostfeld states, "There is still plenty of room in the field for the psychologist, the sociologist, the internist, the psychiatrist, and the epidemiologist, but there is no room for further ineffective studies."

Historically the field had great expectations for a potential breakthrough when the journal *Psychosomatic Medicine* was established in 1939 based on the "specificity theory" of Franz Alexander, who contended that each of seven diseases (bronchial asthma, rheumatoid arthritis, ulcerative colitis, essential hypertension, neurodermatitis, thyrotoxicosis, and duodenal peptic ulcer) were aroused by unexpressible specific emotions. Only the vegetative components were present in overfunctional action leading ultimately to morphological change. For years the journal was inundated by reports of psychoanalytic investigations confirming this specificity.

The failure of this theory and its derived hypotheses stimulated me to develop an alternative theory and a blueprint for action which others adopted to some degree. My own work attempted to use the blueprint for action during the next eighteen years.

The idea that a unique personality type or a specific intrapsychic conflict was essential to the development of a psychosomatic disease can no longer be entertained. But new methods and sophisticated apparatus were necessary to establish general relationships between stress stimuli and biological responses. The literature was then inundated with physiological and biochemical research which was weakly related to clinical problems.

From the bibliography of our own research it may be seen that two areas of study have concerned us. Correlations between the physiological and psychological systems have been more important than linear "cause and effect" concepts. First, there is the general response to stress stimuli with or without conscious emotional arousal, without differentiation, among the primary affects of anxiety, anger, depression or pleasure. The general response is largely within the pituitary-adrenocortical axis and suggests a preparatory facilitation of stress responders. Second, there are the specific, more or less, localized responses which are individually specific ("response specificity") which occur no matter what the stimulus may be. It may be constitutional, inherited, or acquired early by conditioning experiences. At any rate, these are unique for psychological patterns. What is psychological is the subject's appraisal of the meaning (dangerous or not) of stimuli to his comfort, integrity, or very existence and how he defends himself against false interpretation of these meanings. But he does know that, whatever the meaning, he reacts in his personal way, whether this be diarrhea, sweating, tachycardia or tremor.

Of necessity this falls under the overall umbrella of systems theory. In using systems approach we have stressed the relationship between soma and psyche in maturation and development and applied it to concepts of so-called psychosomatic diseases. How do early experiences become imprinted on both psyche and soma, reappearing as related defects in both in the process of dedifferentiation? Research on a group of healthy young males developed a number of variables within the total transactional field which contribute to mental health. These include: physical health, average intelligence, adequate affection and communication in the family, fair discipline, early work experiences, sound ideals and goal-seeking rather than goal-changing. The end-result contributed to adaptation within a specified environment.

The health-illness system cannot be separated to define health and illness each in absolute terms. Health is dependent on factors such as age, culture and social attitudes, internal compensations, defenses, coping, etc. In general, health is maintained when strains affecting one part of the biopsychological system are compensated or counteracted by other parts.

In general, the health-illness system involving body and mind extends from the genetic to the socio-cultural and encompasses development and decline including birth, infancy, childhood, adolescence, young adulthood, maturity, aging, dying and death. Each phase has its characteristic internal processes and its specific stresses and capacities for defense, coping and reconstitution. Each and the whole have their interfaces with specific socio-cultural environments, their ecosystems. This concept transcends disciplinary lines; it combines knowledge of laboratory procedures, life in pairs, families, groups, and the larger society. It is concerned with phases of stability, stress-responses, and despair.

Stages in the life cycle considered as a system may be viewed in several ways. For example in one manner we may view sub-systems including genetics (bioamines), family (communications), experience (trauma), as parts of ontogeny all leading to health or illness and degrees of susceptibility to the latter and coping devices for the former.

In another manner the stages can be enumerated as follows: 1) the relatively undifferentiated neonate; 2) the phases of differentiation or learning through imprinting, reinforcement, imitation, identification, etc; 3) the phase of specific personality and coping development; 4) the phase of health, including proneness to disease; 5) the phase of disease; 6) the phase of chronic illness; and 7) the phase of dying and death.

After much time, energy and work we began to understand that a variety of stress stimuli could produce not only general adaptational mechanisms, but also specific responses in individuals. The theory of response specificity was thus developed and had to include the wide number of sub-systems that preceded and contributed to classes of responses.

Roy R. Grinker, Sr.

July, 1973

Psychosomatic
CONCEPTS

"Human physiology comprises the reciprocal actions and relations of mental and bodily phenomena, as they make up the totality of life.——Scarcely can we have a morbid affection of body in which some feeling or function of mind is not concurrently engaged—directly or indirectly —as cause or as effect."

Henry Holland (1852)

CHAPTER ONE

Introduction

WITHIN little more than a decade, the term "psychosomatic medicine" has become an integral part of the vocabularies of most physicians and many informed laymen. Psychosomatic concepts have infiltrated with varying degrees of accuracy into contemporary intellectual discussions. As a diagnostic approach, a therapeutic attitude, or an etiological concept of disease, the psychosomatic or comprehensive view of man's ills has fired the imaginations of countless physicians and stimulated the curiosity of many research workers in this country. The American Psychosomatic Society has developed a forum for scientific discussions and organized an outstanding professional journal. Both of these have rapidly become important to American medicine since 1939.

The rapid acceptance of psychosomatic concepts was partly the consequence of World War II, during which the somatic effects of excessive anxiety were clearly demonstrated to millions of men under stress and to their medical attendants. However, the public and many of its physicians had already arrived at a stage of sophistication and need which supplied fertile soil for the first assumptions of psychogenesis of bodily disturbances and for the tentative correlations between some emotional conflicts and some somatic diseases. Little as we may now wish to preserve the word "psychosomatic," which calls attention to, rather than denying, mind-body dichotomy, wide usage forces us to preserve it as a symbol of contemporary concepts pertaining to transactions among psychological and somatic systems.

After World War II, many physicians sought training within a hypothetical specialty of psychosomatic medicine, unaware that "psychosomatic" means a conceptual approach to *relationships*, not new physiological or psychological theories or new therapeutic approaches to illness. Enthusiasm for the creation of a new specialty, widespread loose application of superficial psychological interpretations, and formulations of exclusively emotional etiology for somatic disturbances were serious complications of wide and premature dissemination of tentative hypotheses. Uncontrolled conclusions based on incomplete studies of only a few examples of specific syndromes were applied to all cases. The enthusiastic quest for knowledge by a plethora of postwar graduate students seduced their gratified teachers into throwing caution to the winds, into stirring up even more interest among physicians, and into making doubtful therapeutic promises to laymen through popular lectures and articles of questionable accuracy. All this had a devitalizing effect on the scientific aspects of psychosomatic medicine.

Far more serious for the patient was the acceptance by internists and psychiatrists of labeled syndromes as diagnostic categories, serving to evoke psychological pronouncements of etiology and prognosis without reference to the specific forces at work within and around the individual patient. For example, a patient with a peptic ulcer is often interviewed with the intent of eliciting data concerned with early frustration of oral needs. These errors in practice were only secondary to the formalization of early theoretical concepts and their constant reiteration. A lack of critical challenge to the few existing theories has made assumptions seem unassailable and hypotheses capable only of confirmation. As a result, psychosomatic formulations have become stereotypes into which each patient's life history and situation is molded by special focusing, selective interpretation, and omission or neglect of the incongruent.

Within the conceptual aspects of the psychosomatic field two polarities of emphasis have developed, each of great historical significance and of pedagogical effectiveness. The first concept long antedates the modern psychosomatic approach; and, viewed in retrospect, it was an important precursor and foundation. This was the theoretical holistic, global, or total concept, which asserted the unity of mind and body and held that psychic and somatic phenomena are two aspects of the same process. More specifically applied to medicine, every disease is psychosomatic and there is no logical distinction between mind and body, nor between the mental and the physical. Applied to physiology, mood and intellect differ from other physiological processes only in complexity, and not fundamentally in quality.

These holistic concepts, promulgated long ago by philosophers, have stood the test of time and the progress of science. They have served to loosen the departmentalization of knowledge and to create dissatisfaction with explanations of total organismic function as a sum of part-functions of related organs, and have catalyzed the development of a comprehensive approach for all the biological sciences, especially for medicine and psychiatry. However, holistic concepts in operation require that the position of the observer be outside the organism, which handicaps the analysis of development and action of inner part-functions in transactional processes,* which has been the central problem of medicine. Furthermore, viewing "the patient as a whole" is impossible, for in such attempts the patient becomes a part in transaction with other individuals, including the observer, society, culture, etc. Even though holism has been a necessary advance in thinking, it requires detachment from the approach it is utilized to serve. Detailed study of what constitutes psychosomatic unity requires more than distance from which the organism can only be observed as a unit. What is truly the subject matter of psychosomatic medicine includes the processes within and between the many systems which effect such unity. This requires the detailed analysis of quantity, timing, and reciprocity of function of many parts which accomplish

* For a definition and clarification of transactional processes see chapter X, especially page 155. The position of the observer and what is observed is discussed in chapter IV.

integration, furnish substitutive or emergency functions, and delay, resist, or modify disintegrative forces. Our central interest is in those functions and mechanisms which develop, preserve, defend, or restore wholeness. However, the relationship of parts maintaining balance can be studied without losing the vision of total integration as a natural phenomenon of open living systems.

The opposite polarity of current emphasis has dealt with an extremely limited and sharply defined field of observation. In order to exclude consideration of ideas symbolized in conversion symptoms, expressed by organs innervated by the voluntary nervous system, only the vegetative nervous system and the organs it innervates are selected as the subject matter of psychosomatic medicine by many investigators. Their basic assumption is that feelings and emotions are subjective expressions of concomitant activity only of the vegetative nervous system. Health or disease then depends upon the degree of strain or tension put upon inner organs by factors that influence quantity, duration, and direction of vegetative innervation. This approach is concerned with the vicissitudes of specific feelings as they directly affect specific inner organs or systems, to result in overstrain, producing disturbance of function and eventually breakdown of tissues.

Many doubts have been entertained as to the logic behind the placing of voluntary and vegetative nervous systems in opposition for the expression of ideas and feelings, and as to the emphasis on specificity of emotions in influencing specific function of organs in health and disease. It has been this emphasis that has created the clinical stereotypes with insufficient data from individuals and with deficient statistical verification. The conceptual basis of the doctrine of specificity and the methodology behind it will be discussed in detail later. Now it is only important to state that just as the holistic concepts are too vague and detached, so the specificity hypotheses are too narrow and too limited to a special area of transaction, with little regard for an indefinite number of intervening variables. Instead, a tremendous jump from feelings to organ dysfunction becomes necessary to satisfy a bias which is essentially medical—concerned with causes of diseases and with their treatment —and not physiological or psychophysiological.

Both the global and specifistic concepts greatly stimulated interest and development in psychosomatic medicine, yet each in its own way in time obstructed further progress. Without depreciating their historical value and their significance in pedagogy, I feel that their repetition does not serve to increase our understanding of fundamental psychosomatic processes. In my opinion what is needed now is a clear and succinct statement of the assumptions, hypotheses, and available methodology on which further research may be based. Toward that end I shall first critically outline the chief historical and current theoretical positions and the accepted contemporary methods of investigation, and then indicate certain possibilities which are available for the future.

CHAPTER TWO

Historical Concepts

PROGRESS in science and medicine and, for that matter, even in individual growth and learning, seems to make sudden spurts, like mutations, evidenced by some new discovery or new way of thinking, hailed as a milestone or the beginning of a new epoch. Such a new era began in 1935 with the publication of Dunbar's *Emotions and Bodily Changes*, in which the world's available literature (2251 articles) reporting on relationships between somatic functions and feelings, was collected, abstracted, and synthesized. This marked the beginning of a formalized approach to comprehensive medicine. There followed rapidly a systematization of concepts and procedures, the establishment of scientific societies, the founding of a special journal, and the development of departments and institutes within universities and hospitals, all under the rubric of psychosomatic medicine.

Once these events occurred, the historically curious began to trace the roots of ideas that seemed so new and startling to this generation. Much evidence accumulated to indicate that many outstanding thinkers, investigators, and clinicians had, in the long past, touched on many fundamental and tangential aspects of what we now call psychosomatic medicine. The term itself was discovered to be a product of the last century (Stainbrook, 1952). Some cynically contend by a process of retrospective reinterpretation of what was meant by writers of the past (Bernard, 1865; Darwin, 1871; Jennings, 1905, 1906), in terms of what we now know, that there is nothing new under the sun. Others contend that such complete accreditation of priority to historical work can only be the result of incorrectly loose and liberal interpretations.

The truth probably lies somewhere in between. Both direct and indirect expressions, explicit and implicit concepts, may be found throughout the history of science indicating that psychosomatic, comprehensive, or unitary thinking about mind-body relations in health and disease existed in rudimentary and sometimes sophisticated form. Certainly there can be no more complete and succinct statement of psychosomatic medicine today than that formulated by Henry Holland in 1852—just one hundred years ago. What was lacking in the past, and seemed to develop suddenly, was attempts at systematization of these ideas, formulation of specific hypotheses, and a methodology applicable for fresh investigations. Since it is the modern systematized theoretical positions which I wish to analyze critically, I will briefly discuss some of their historical homologues.

In the available literature of ancient medicine, whether Egyptian, Hebraic, or Greek, there may be found many references to the mind-body problem with emphasis on the causative factors for mental disorders emanating from the body. A healthy mind was presumed to exist only in a healthy body, whose humoral variations presumably influenced psychological states. The phlegmatic, sanguine, choleric, and melancholic temperaments were the first personality profiles which were considered to be dependent upon specific somatic factors. Western civilization, through its philosophers, has always indicated a preoccupation with the mind-body or soul-body relationship. The answers to this problem have varied with the prevailing cultural trends and emphasis has swung from mind to body and back again. Many serious thinkers considered mind and body but two aspects of the same process perceived differently according to the position of the observer. It has taken science and psychiatry a long time to reach this degree of sophistication, for the writings of even the recent past indicate clearly that most scientific observers have been oriented toward viewing linear relationships in only one direction.

The pathologists, especially the neuropathologists, attempted to find the "cause" of mental diseases and morbid fears in structural changes of the body, particularly in the brain and within its ganglion cells. Not only was specificity of neuronal changes as the basis of clinical psychiatric entities undemonstrable, but also specific alterations could not be correlated with time, degree, or locus of any disease process (Grinker, 1934). Von Monakow (1925) ascribed the cause of mental disorders to disturbances of filtration through the choroid plexus which permits toxins to pass through the hemo-encephalic barrier into the nervous system. A modern attempt at transmutation of these hypotheses of specific cellular etiology into the histochemical field is now similarly failing (Hyden and Hartelius, 1948).

Bechterew in 1911 was able to demonstrate in the cerebral cortex nervous centers which control peripheral vegetative functions. His physiological work has been extensively modified and amplified by Fulton and others (1938). If these centers really control the function of the internal organs, then naturally, central lesions could produce discrete peripheral pathology or dysfunction. Many years later Harvey Cushing (1932) demonstrated that chronic visceral disturbances such as peptic ulcer and bowel intussusception could be produced by focal lesions of the diencephalon and prefrontal lobes respectively. Since disturbances of the visceral organs are the special interest of the first psychosomatic approach, these neurogenic hypotheses assumed great importance, even though they dealt with physiological mechanisms, to the neglect of the etiological role of feelings in health and illness, unaccompanied by central lesions. Clearly demonstrated was the fact that any level of the nervous system, from peripheral vegetative outflow to cerebral cortical centers, may be concerned, along with humoral processes, in maintaining internal equilibrium.

The experimental physiologists within the psychological disciplines measured exactly the activities of the special senses and the peripheral vegetative nervous system innervating vasomotor and sudomotor activities in the skin. These physiological processes were correlated with crude classifications of personality types or psychiatric diagnoses. The results were not meaningful in a specific sense except to indicate that variability of peripheral function did co-exist with emotional changes.

It was not until Pavlov (1928) developed his technique of applying carefully measured and timed stimuli to animals on whom visceral functions, such as salivary secretion, could be measured that physiological processes and behavior could be experimentally correlated. His conditioned-reflex theory developed from the fact that internal behavior could be stimulated, modified, and perpetuated through the formation of functional patterns, facilitated or inhibited by external stimuli. Only later was the significance of previously uncontrolled emotional stimuli recognized, leading, in the hands of American students of conditioned reflexes, to the conclusion that feeling relationship between animal and human observer also affected visceral activity (Anderson and Liddell, 1935). Although the conditioned-reflex theory is now liberally applied to human phenomena, proof of the capacity for conditioning even of the human infant is still not satisfactory. David Levy (1952) has recently advocated animal observation and experimentation to provide the supplementary data necessary for conclusions regarding early psychosomatic processes.

Somewhat later, Cannon (1932) studied the effects of strong emotional stimuli on the visceral activity of experimental animals and demonstrated the mechanisms by which the animal mobilizes its resources for emergency fight or flight. He amplified Claude Bernard's concept of stability of the internal milieu or homeostasis, and demonstrated many mechanisms and functions concerned in avoiding or combating internal disequilibrium. Cannon's work has also been directly applied to human physiology and psychosomatic approaches, although in many instances mechanisms clearly described in cats are not found in humans, i.e. emergency rise of blood sugar.

The investigations of both Pavlov and Cannon have become basic for the development of psychosomatic concepts. They clearly demonstrated that needs or hunger, and fear or anticipation of danger, could evoke severe, immediate, or long-standing physiological disturbances within the nervous system and its innervated organs. Recently Selye (1946) has emphasized the role of the pituitary and adrenocortical endocrine systems in reaction to physical and emotional stress, producing acute shocklike responses and long-standing adaptations. Thus, added to the purely mechanistic and physiological considerations of internal processes, symbolic representations of need or stress were recognized as important influences which affected the organism's stability and which stimulated processes concerned with equilibrium, adaptation, and learning.

In a study of humans, the scientific constitutionalists, beginning with Kretschmer (1930), observed the correlation of static bodily types with physical and mental abnormalities.

From these findings ulcer, hypertension, asthma, and such vague entities as schizophrenia and manic-depressive psychoses, were correlated with one of three fixed body types. Concepts in the constitutional field had not yet transcended the anatomical to include function, particularly functions of a biochemical nature. Despite the early abandonment of these vague correlations, Sheldon (1940) recently revived the concept of somatic destiny, and Morris (1948), the philosopher, has extended it to personality types. George Draper (1924) utilized variations in bodily types in making direct correlations with several somatic dysfunctions that are now called psychosomatic diseases. Even though his findings were not convincing, his work greatly stimulated Dunbar and ushered in what may be termed the formalized era of a psychosomatic approach.

It can be assumed that detailed studies of the writings of many of the leaders in medicine of the last hundred years indicated recognition of the relationship between emotional disturbances and physical illness in some casual phrase or in such general terms as fatigue and nervousness (Holland, 1852). But von Bergman (1913) is credited with first considering that peptic ulcer may result from disturbances within the vegetative nervous system and that these could be produced by emotional stress. In discussing peripheral mechanisms, Alkan (1930) suggested that tissue infections may result from arterial spasm initiated by emotional stress. He anticipated some current concepts when he stated that inner dangers, signaled by anxiety, decrease overt action and therefore diminish discharge or expression of nervous tension to an inadequate level. When tension is expressed only in fantasy, because the effort of discharge is blocked, the effect may be spasm of blood vessels and eventually tissue damage.

All these investigations did not take cognizance of the emotional reactions of human subjects either as stimuli or concurrent phenomena to somatic processes, or as the results of physiological states. The existing methods of observation and recording did not then reveal the specific feelings aroused by external stimuli or stresses. It was not until the psychology developed by Freud and his followers became more widely known that a conceptual scheme and an operational tool became available for the detection and measurement of these feelings.

The beginning of psychoanalysis and its later development brought unconscious dynamic factors into etiological consideration as against the classical personality typology and the nosological classification of psychiatric entities. Freud's libido theory, although now considerably altered, was the beginning of the understanding of somatic effects on mental and emotional life, since libido was simply a force or energy derived from bodily functions. The first theory of anxiety was psychosomatic in that blocking of sexual activity was presumed to generate noxious substances within the gonadal system. Later, anxiety was considered as a signal which detonated repressive and often regressive forces that shunted expression of psychological drives from higher-level verbal or behavioral paths into old infantile patterns. Many of these involved increased activity of internal organs. Thus, psychoanalysis developed for the first time a dynamic circular concept of relationship between mind and body. On its hypotheses psychosomatic medicine, or what Freud called "the future of medicine," could develop.

Earlier Alfred Adler (1912) had located the somatic symptoms in neurotic patients at the site of a constitutional organ inferiority. From this defect, and the inferiority accompanying early childhood weakness and dependency, Adler derived character and personality as the resultant of efforts to overcompensate and develop a feeling of mastery over the environment. Felix Deutsch (1922), a Freudian psychoanalyst, later considered that organ neuroses develop at the focus of a previous disease process—for example, asthma developing in persons who had suffered from severe pertussis. The later works of Deutsch (1949) and many other psychoanalysts indicate that they attributed physical symptoms from organs innervated by the vegetative nervous system to a symbolic representation of a repressed emotion. In fact, Karl Menninger (1938), in his discussion of internalized hate, frequently mentioned disease of internal organs as representing partial suicide. Finally, Alexander (1935–36), a psychoanalyst with a biological background, began to utilize broader psychoanalytic concepts in a context of more generalized physiological principles. His influence in the last two decades has stirred in medicine and psychiatry a new hope of synthesis.

It is obvious that this brief sketch of some precursors of psychosomatic medicine from several scientific disciplines has not done justice to any. I have only tried to indicate those contributions which showed a trend toward elucidating anatomical and physiological mechanisms connecting emotions and somatic function, whether the emphasis was in one direction or the other. Not until Freudian psychology developed those dynamic concepts embodied in the libido theory and those basic to the fusion and defusion of instincts, which ascribed the energy of mental life to somatic sources and disturbances in somatic function to unconscious mental processes, could a dynamic circular transactional concept of mind and body develop.

The roots of modern psychosomatic medicine are physiological, derived from the investigations of Pavlov, Cannon, and their students, and psychological, derived from psychoanalytic theory. Pursuance of both lines of investigation independently and concurrently, each with its own methods, and finding some means by which both fields may be viewed and studied simultaneously as properties of a single integrated whole, constitute the subject matter of much-needed psychosomatic investigations. It is the development and functioning of patterns of relationship among somatic and psychological systems that properly defines the psychosomatic study that is evolving in our time.

CHAPTER THREE

Current Conceptual Models

FOLLOWING her initial compilation of the psychosomatic literature, Dunbar continued her own work in the special direction of developing psychological profiles characteristic of specific disease syndromes. Before describing these profiles and their method of elicitation it may be worth while to examine her general principles (Dunbar, 1943).

She states that bodily changes may be brought about not only by bacterial organisms and toxins, but also by mental stimuli and emotions. Inadequate expression or solution of emotional conflicts occurs usually when they are not due to external causes. When expressive action is inappropriate or inadequate, the emotion and its physiological accompaniments disturb the organism by creating permanent tensions, which produce persistent or recurrent disorders in function. Problems excluded from consciousness are short-circuited into subcortical mechanisms. Thus Dunbar uses, explicitly, applications to psychology from the first two physical laws of thermodynamics, as laws of "emotional thermodynamics." Psychic energy, not expressed through higher levels, seeks its outlet through physical symptoms;

hence energy is conserved. The second law is rephrased to state that if such symptoms are the result of permanent structural damage, energy is correspondingly dissipated and made unavailable. Thus, somatic dysfunction is "a waste or dissipation of energy due to the faulty design of the personality."

This faulty design is an organismic-environmental constellation of factors peculiar to specific syndromes of somatic dysfunction. Dunbar has developed a system of obtaining psychosomatic case histories for the uncovering of these factors, including free association, reporting of somatic sensations, and other special techniques of examination. A fairly complete picture of the longitudinal behavior pattern against the background of the significant physical and human environment is obtained. With these facts, an American personality profile characteristic of specific psychosomatic entities is constructed and, according to Dunbar, statistically verifiable for each group in from 80 to 100 per cent of cases. The criteria for her profiles include heredity, personal data, previous health, accident record, general adjustment and characteristic behavior pattern, areas of focal conflict and character reactions.

To epitomize and highlight the personality characteristics for the syndromes under study, Dunbar uses single phrases as follows: the accident-prone are "hobos"; sufferers from coronary occlusion and hypertension are "top-dogs" or "would-be-top-dogs"; from anginal syndromes, "prima donnas" or "big frogs in little puddles"; from rheumatic fever and rheumatic heart disease "teachers' pets" and "martyrs"; from cardiac arrhythmias "children in the dark"; and diabetics are "muddlers." The profiles are concluded to be of diagnostic, prognostic, and therapeutic significance.

Before analyzing Dunbar's theoretical position, the profile formulations should first be considered. They have not been sufficiently checked against a large group of healthier subjects and against sufferers from other psychosomatic syndromes. The profile summaries are so similar, because so many general factors are included in them, that other observers have difficulty in making the necessary discriminations, much less anywhere near the same statistically significant correlations. Personality profiles have been intuitively recognized by the great internists of the past whose acute observations taught them the kinds of diseases that more often attack certain types of people, often determined by little signs exposed during examination. Dunbar has attempted to extend and formalize these observations. However, her methods, although definable and scientific, are not capable of penetrating beneath the surface of an individual's mask and exposing the fundamental conflicts, the inexpressible emotions and their effects. Although life situations and environmental factors can be elicited, only the most superficial defenses and reaction formations of the patient can be described by her methods. However, just as in the obsessive-compulsive personality, which has developed rigid and ritualistic defenses against underlying hostilities, the meaning, type, and direction of these aggressions and their proximity to consciousness remain unknown until the primary processes are uncovered. It should be mentioned that those psychoanalysts who have most severely criticized Dunbar's superficial data have themselves not penetrated much deeper into the essential psychodynamic processes, but are also dealing with defenses, albeit at a deeper level.

Having seen that the operational procedures by which profiles are determined are inadequate for their conceived purpose, and the resulting data too generalized, we may now examine Dunbar's conceptual model. It is highly mechanistic, dealing in variable distribution of energy which is often disturbed by internal difficulties preventing adequate expression of feelings stirred up by life situations. Factors concerned in such difficulties may only be surmised by the reaction formations against them which are included in the profile, and these negative aspects cannot be considered as positive factors of etiology. With the absence of more direct expression of action, the organ of preparation for such action must carry the task of dealing with the resulting tension or accumulation of energy, discharging it in dysfunction or succumbing to morphological change and "wasting" it. For the latter concept there is no proof, only inaccurate analogy to physics. The reversibility of tissue damage, the alternation of dysfunction among the organs, and the frequent reciprocal relationship with psychoses are overlooked. There is no clear explanation as to the significance of specific profiles in relation to special syndromes or to special defects in expression causing appropriate organs to carry the brunt of the short-circuited energy. The faulty design is ascribed to interaction with recent and current life situations; any consideration of the total organism as a psychosomatic process in time is slighted. In fact, despite her theoretical statements we find nowhere in her procedures any examination of varying physiological states or studies of basic emotional processes; hence these cannot be correlated. Finally, personality profiles and disease syndromes of internal organs cannot be logically considered as two aspects of the same phenomena, since the disease is considered as a stereotype and the profile a statistic in Dunbar's hands. The resulting impasse will continue no matter how much more the profile pattern is refined.

Franz Alexander has, during the last twenty years, contributed more to the psychosomatic field than any other investigator, both directly and through his influence on students and colleagues. His theories were not mentioned first for the sake of chronology, yet Dunbar's later writings and those of most other contemporary workers reflect Alexander's influence in modifying their original formulations. Reference is made to two books that contain the essentials of Alexander's viewpoint (Alexander and French, 1948; Alexander, 1950). Certain of his general statements should be presented before outlining his particular theories.

Psychological processes in the present stage of our knowledge should be studied by psychological methods and reported exactly, not in general terms such as anxiety, tension, etc. Correlations between psyche and soma should not be made between personality types and somatic processes;

rather, the psychic aspects should be studied in terms of the individual and of his specific emotional problems. Alexander, most clearly of all psychiatrists, verbalizes two-way or circular psychosomatic assumptions when he states that psychological processes are physiological phenomena that are communicated verbally (here he ignores any preverbal psychology), and that all bodily functions are affected by psychological states. The psyche functions through the physiological and is not something apart from the body.

Alexander's theoretical model may be succinctly expressed as follows:

1. All healthy and sick human functions are psychosomatic.

2. Emotions are always associated with concomitant action patterns expressed through a portion of the autonomic nervous system and its innervated organs.

3. For specific emotions there are appropriate concomitant vegetative patterns.

4. Emotions repressed from overt expression lead to chronic tensions, thus intensifying in degree and prolonging in time the concomitant vegetative innervation.

5. The resulting excessive organ innervation leads to disturbance of function which may eventually end in morphological changes in the tissues.

By Alexander's definition, unlike hysterical conversion symptoms, which were assumed to be symbolic expressions of emotional tension; psychosomatic disturbances, in the narrower sense of the word, are vegetative responses associated with chronic emotional states. As Saul (1939) puts the concept: The nervous system is like a hydrostatic system; when the emotional level of energy is dammed up by voluntary inhibition the discharge occurs through the vegetative nervous system. Alexander's original studies on disturbances of the gastrointestinal system led him to postulate conflict situations leading to "emotional syllogisms" corresponding to vectors of intake and output. Gastric dyspepsia and peptic ulcer are related to conflict over the wish to receive or to take; diarrhea over the wish to give or to eliminate; constipation over the wish to retain. Some years later Alexander (1950, Figure 1) considered the conflict situations to be more complicated and more universal, as evidenced by his current circular schematization of human personality. This he has graphically portrayed as a circle beginning with the universal human need for dependency and proceeding in an orderly process of chain reactions, returning to the original dependency. Dependency interfered with leads to narcissistic protest and overcompensation, which in turn results in effort and competitive aggressiveness. This produces anxiety or guilt with regression to dependency, the original point of departure. Alexander states that if direct outlets for dependency needs are blocked by external or internal forces, the energy is expressed through the parasympathetic nervous system, which corresponds to the conserving, building-up, anabolic processes. If effort and aggressiveness are blocked, the flow then proceeds through the sympathetic nervous system. Because there are various ways of expressing the nuances of each of these trends, there are various physiological innervations corresponding to them. Thus, from the "dependency-parasympathetic" arc, ulcer, constipation, diarrhea, colitis, asthma, etc. may be the resulting dysfunctions. The "effort-sympathetic" arc may contribute to the production of arthritis, hypertension, migraine, hyperthyroidism, diabetes, etc.

From Alexander's theoretical concepts the block which shunts psychological energy into the vegetative pathways should be at a psychological level. Saul (1939) states that the block is in the nature of "voluntary inhibition," by which he means unconscious psychological inhibition of utilization of voluntary pathways. Grinker (1939) has suggested conditioned inhibition or higher-level extinction. However, Alexander diagrams the position of the block on the efferent arc of a portion of the autonomic nervous system, forcing the energy of expression to adopt another autonomic pathway leading to neuro-endocrinic excitation affecting specific organs. If we are dealing with psychological processes of repression, their neurological counterparts should be at higher levels; and if we speak of lower-level blocks on the vegetative net, we must have an adequate and exclusively physiological explanation. Neither of these is present in Alexander's hypothesis.

However, Alexander does not subscribe to a monistic concept of causality, for he lists nine etiological categories from heredity to later-life emotional experiences in intimate personal relations. Furthermore, he cautions that the symptom is only one part of a neurotic disturbance of the personality, and he is still more cautious in stating that morphological changes occur from a specific psychodynamic pattern only if a constitutional or x factor is likewise present.

Alexander states that psychological processes can be studied adequately only by psychological methods—not, for example, by electroencephalography. We should add that in these days physiological processes and disorders also deserve appropriate methods for their observation and measurement, as precise and as dynamic as the psychoanalytic methods and formulations. This same precision is necessary in describing and evaluating early cultural and social factors concerned in etiology and later-life situations involved in precipitation. Therefore, such physiological measurements as sphygmomanometer readings of blood pressure or urinary-sugar estimations, as well as social observations expressed as "frustrated dependency" or "early forcing of independent activities," as utilized by Alexander, represent neither adequate nor accurate evaluation of physiological or social systems. It seems that most psychiatrists, physiologists, or social scientists are too deeply specialized and immersed in their own disciplines to be able to observe accurately the relationships or bridges to other disciplines involved in studying co-variables. Each, however, should indicate when and where his observations lose their sharpness and when other specialists at different positions in the total field are necessary (cf. Chapter XI).

That vegetative responses are involved in expressions of emotional states can be accepted in general, but we must be careful of the human tendency to dichotomize in exaggerating the contrast between voluntary nervous activity regulating relations with the external world and autonomic nervous functions dominating internal affairs, and between parasympathetic conserving and sympathetic discharging activities. Neither dichotomy withstands close scrutiny. Instead, both voluntary-involuntary and parasympathetic-sympathetic processes are in constant phasic and co-operative activity. Actually and symbolically the organism as a whole and its parts are constantly in "fight and flight," in anabolism and catabolism of all gradations, varying with each moment.

There is an inconsistency in dismissing the voluntary nervous system from consideration of psychosomatic disturbances and then dealing with vectors applicable to the gastrointestinal tract, correlating the wish to receive or to take and the wish to give or to retain with mouth and anal sphincter activities respectively, both of which are innervated by the voluntary nervous system. In contrast to a favorite formulation of Alexander which represents diarrhea as a correlate of an unconscious wish to give, actual observations indicate that this physiological disturbance does not primarily reside in the excretory functions, but may be associated with decreased reverse peristalsis of the large bowel, increased emptying time of the small bowel, intensification of the gastrocolic reflex (Szasz, 1952), or gastric dumping, etc. In fact, from increased lacrimal and nasal secretion to failure of fluid absorption in the caecum, the entire gastrointestinal tract is functionally deranged in states of diarrhea. In 1852, Holland wrote: "Primary causes of disease are often wholly obscured by those of secondary kind. Organs remote from each other by place and function are simultaneously disturbed. Translations of morbid action take place from one part to another." This points up the fallacy of relying on observations of single functions or of overemphasizing the presenting complaint of the patient as the significant somatic expression of emotional disturbances. It opens to question the entire assumption that a specific vegetative activity is normally concomitant with a specific feeling, and that repression or inhibition of the feelings leads to accentuation in degree and time of the usual vegetative concomitant, resulting then in dysfunction and tissue change.

Although Szasz (1952) agrees with Alexander as to the leading role the vegetative nervous system plays in psychosomatic disorders, he speaks less of concomitant innervations (to specific emotions) and more of "regressive innervation." This is a specific, localized, parasympathetic hyperactivity which is currently pathological although it was, in the past, appropriate to a level of growth. Sympathetic vegetative discharges are appropriate if entirely expended; they become pathological if chronically maintained. Although the concept of regression adheres to the facts, the significance of parasympathetic activity as older or primary is not clear.

Alexander's graphic representation of internal forces applicable to all humans and deranged in sufferers from psychosomatic disorders as circular is misleading. His is not a truly circular, two-way or self-corrective model except if viewed in long spans of developmental time. It is lineal, and it is not subject to internal or external spontaneously self-corrective processes—as Alexander himself indicates when he states that environmental factors are only precipitating. The pulsations around the circle can only beat faster or slower; the process is on a single track. Such circus movements are characteristic for late-developing characterological defenses which are far removed from primary psychological processes and hence unmodifiable by the free energy of the drives or by learning from fresh life experiences. Although consisting of unconscious character traits uncovered only by psychoanalytic procedures, they are still very close to the personality profiles of Dunbar. The monotonous formulations of dependency, frustration, and aggression, even though juggled into so-called specific dynamic configurations, are unsharp universals. They are so far removed from processes influencing psyche and soma when both constitute a relatively undifferentiated system that they can only be considered as characterological precipitates derived from these action processes or in reaction to them.

One of the outstanding psychosomatic researches of recent years has been carried on by Therese Benedek (1952b). In her work on psychosexual functions in women, each subject was under close psychological scrutiny by the method of psychoanalysis, while daily vaginal smears and basal body temperature as indices of ovarian function were simultaneously obtained, independently and without communication by an endocrinologist. Only a year later were the daily psychological and endocrinological states correlated in the presence of a third person. The psychoanalyst was able, from her data, to reach a high level of predictability as to the hormonal activity, so that there was a correlation between each hormonal variation of the sexual cycle and its psychodynamic manifestation. The emotional cycle was parallel to the hormonal cycle, and both together constituted the so-called sexual cycle. The result justified the clear-cut conclusion that the sexual cycle is a psychosomatic unit. The psychological work was later expanded into analyses of the psychosomatic aspects of pregnancy, mother-child symbiosis, and the climacterium.

Benedek's theoretical concepts are clearly expressed in terms of systems of energy. The instinctual, somatically derived energy, after the many vicissitudes in development, forms and maintains the personality upon which the free energy of the drives exerts constant stimulation. Benedek's reformulation of Freud's early libido theory may be directly quoted as follows: "Thus Freud indicated the anaclitic nature of sexual energy; the maturation as well as the function of the sexual instinct depends upon the processes which maintain the self, i.e. upon the manifestations of the ego instincts. In early infancy, there is a period during which only ego instincts—only physiology—is evident; then follows a period during which the developing libidinous energy appears fused with the energy of ego instincts. (The object of both is the same: mother-nourishment-self.) Only after significant developmental differentiation can the two types of instinctual energy be recognized as opposing forces. From that (developmental) time on, there exists an ever-present possibility of conflict between the opposing tendencies; these partake, in turn, in the further developmental processes of the personality." (1953).

Freud later dealt with the fusion and defusion of antagonistic forces (life and death instincts) as unconscious and repetitive participants in the organization and function of the psychic apparatus. Further integration of physiological energies with unconscious psychic processes leads to the development of preconscious needs, experienced as pleasure or pain, and subject to control by the ego. It is then that these forces become the motivating tendencies of conscious, goal-directed behavior and conscious affects. Benedek has shown in her studies on female sex hormones that the physiological factors which influence the distribution and discharge of energy in the ego can be observed and measured psychoanalytically. By this method those forces participating in the formation of personality can be differentiated from the psychic tensions created currently by

new, changed, or intensified sources. The day-by-day fluctuations in emotional expression can be gauged against the
permanent motivation of the personality; and the current
emotional state and behavior can be interpreted in terms
of the motivating psychodynamic tendencies which in turn
can be correlated with fluctuations of the hormones.

Benedek discusses affects as indicators of feeling or
change in psychophysiological equilibrium. The affects or
emotions originate in energies of the physiological processes,
and it is in the unconscious that communication takes
place between physiological energy and mental representations through a "primary process." There is an extreme
variability of possibilities of combinations between the
physiological energies and ideational contents—derivatives,
elaborations, and recombinations.

"Many investigations have dealt with establishing the
parallelism between affect and its physiological accompani-
ment, yet these investigations deal with the external physiology of the affect-response rather than with the problem
of the changes in the instinctual source of stimulation."
Here the author has reference to the fact that a simple relationship between instinctual stimulation and affect-
response can only occur before differentiation of the
psychic apparatus has taken place. Such unmodified discharges under special circumstances leave lasting memory
traces of insecurity, greediness, envy, etc. Benedek contends
that psychoanalysis can follow an affect from the early
psychophysiological need as a diffuse expression of the

mental apparatus until it has become organized as a structuralized part of the personality. She analyzes affects in regard to the psychodynamic tendencies which constitute them, their genetic motivation, their function on the personality, and the internal disequilibrium which activates them. To trace the energy of the affects to their physiological source is a goal of psychosomatic research. The test of Benedek's theoretical position depends upon the confirmation of her work on the female sexual cycle and on further study of the influence of basic physiological events on psychodynamic tendencies and primary affects.

Harold Wolff has been the leader and teacher of a large group of investigators concerned with psychosomatic problems. His theoretical formulations and operational procedures are sufficiently distinct to constitute a special position in the field, perhaps best epitomized by the title of his books and papers—for example, "Life Situations, Emotions and Bodily Change," in which the latter is specified according to the clinical syndromes under discussion. Wolff (1950) points out that stresses which affect man arise not only from his biological and physical environment, but also from threats and symbols of past dangers, from failures and frustrations of his needs and aspirations, and from cultural pressures and rapid social changes. Bodily reactions to stress or attempts at adaptation may be generalized or local and in varying degrees successful.

In most of Wolff's works the life situation was interpreted in terms of the conscious awareness of the patient of his reaction through a process of self-reporting. Although Wolff knows the criticism of this superficial reflection of life situations by those who deal with the unconscious feelings which these stir up, he states that the individuals' degree of awareness is not as important as the basic significance of the situation. He emphasizes the possible variability of response to repeated stimuli—diminution or accentuation—which he attempts to offset by intervening control periods of observation without stress.

Wolff points out that specific dysfunctions are fragmentations of protective reactions, which follow the principle of parsimony, in that specific and localized responses represent adjustments which are not too costly and permit, otherwise, a relatively secure and tranquil existence. He contends that the dominant protective reaction patterns are stockbound, in other words, hereditarily constitutional and, as an afterthought, developmental through early life experiences.

Grace, Wolf, and Wolff report that stressful life situations call forth conscious emotional responses associated with a monotonously similar pattern in the organs reacting—i.e., swelling, hyperemia, hypersecretion, and hypermotility. Such defense reactions are not specific except in terms of the special organs involved; factors concerned with such hypothetical selectivity are not clear. What can be expected from this theoretical position is clearer elucidation of the disordered function of special organs beyond the stereotype of the above-described monotonous pattern, the extension of such studies to yet unapproached organs, and the further clarification of "life situations." However, neither more significant synthesis nor more detailed analysis of instincts, drives, feelings, or affects as they are related to physiological processes can be accomplished by ignoring the individual meaning given to "life situation" on ever deeper levels.

Another step toward a better evaluation of life situations, from earlier settings, in the formation of psychosomatic disturbances has been made by Jurgen Ruesch (1948, 1951). He derives his scientific model for human nature from the theory of communications which considers that events linking parts, whole individuals, groups, and society, are explicable by one conceptual model. Applying this to psychosomatic problems in general, he itemizes several factors:

1. There is unsatisfactory self-expression in interpersonal relations in one or more areas of personality.

2. Perceptive processes related to social events are distorted by preponderance of proprioceptive systems.

3. Perceptive messages are interpreted as coercive.

4. Value judgments are based on inner actions.

5. There is lack of integration and goal.

6. There is poor observation of action in others with little self-corrective process.

7. There is more dependence on others than exchange of information and co-operative interaction.

8. The weight of information comes from chemical and mechanical sense organs and little from mature visual and auditory senses.

9. Bodily signs are more important than symbolism.

10. The delineation of psychological-physiological boundaries is incomplete.

11. There is a magical identity of self with others, and there are no corrective measures.

Using this model, Ruesch has studied several syndromes. Persons suffering from vasospastic disturbances in the peripheral blood vessels are, he finds, very dependent, with a low tolerance for frustration, the reactions to which are expressed within the vegetative nervous system. They show an immaturity or faulty social learning which is based upon an early feeling of lack of continuity and consistency from their parents. There is an absence of consistency in love, reward, and punishment. The result is that the child attempts to control its frustrations rather than to master its environment, and thus develops a poor symbolic self-expression, using its organ responses instead. In other words, the child gets stuck in an immature state of dealing with tension rather than with symbolic systems. In summary, we have a conceptual model which describes the victim of psychosomatic disturbances as suffering a failure in communication, based upon early defects in interactions with his first human environment.

Ruesch's general theoretical position postulates that all

psychosomatic processes occur in individuals who are immature and tend to remain socially isolated because they
did not master the prevailing system of communication of
adulthood. The body becomes the essential instrument of
communication; the origin and destination of messages are
both within the organism. Disease disturbs the instrument
of communication; likewise alteration or arrested development of functions of communication may result in disease.

This is a statement of influences which have emanated
from social forces and have impinged upon the organism
at various ages, derived from data elicited in adult life.
However, the theoretical position so defined becomes un-
operational unless procedures can be developed to study
the action and mechanisms in process at various crucial
times of environmental-organismic transaction. Ruesch
has brilliantly emphasized social forces and the mechanisms
of interpersonal and intrapersonal communication, but we
are left without operational procedures for the definition
and analysis of the receptive, integrative, and defensive
processes.

To extend the concept of environment as a significant
factor in the development of psychosomatic disturbances,
Halliday (1948) has approached the problems of etiology
and mechanism from the viewpoint that it is society that
has the sickness. He notes a rapid social disintegration in
the last fifty years and attributes the resulting deterioration
of child-parent relationships as most significant for the development of chronic recurrent illnesses in which psycho-

logical factors are important. Change in society and increase in social insecurity have resulted in severe disturbances in the children of our day. In the latter part of the nineteenth century children progressed in their "own good time," in a busy, somewhat unhygienic, but permissive environment. They were fed frequently, they were carried in mother's arms, they lay with her in bed, and their toilet training was late. In contrast, rigid schedules were standard in the second and third decade of the twentieth century. Bottle superseded breast, infants were wheeled in buggies and lived in nicely carpeted houses which should not be soiled. The offspring was usually an only child and remained an "only" child even after his siblings were born. Each child became more precious as the family decreased in size. The relationship between husband and wife shifted and more control over the child was exerted. Halliday states that as the birth rate goes down, the frequency of psychosomatic illness rises. Halliday has developed pertinent generalized concepts concerning the effect of social change on rate of incidence of chronic noninfectious, nontraumatic diseases. However, in such a global approach the individual becomes lost and our understanding of process is not furthered.

We have considerable data on the effect of social and cultural attitudes on the types of psychosomatic disturbance as they vary in our country within different ethnic groups. Social anthropologists (Mead, 1947, 1949; Mead and MacGregor, 1951) have attempted to relate differences in

psychosomatic patterns to variations in mother-child relations within a variety of nonliterate societies and within
different family structures of our own society (Henry,
1949, 1951). In our own rapidly moving culture conversion
symptoms and phobias are much less common today than
twenty-five years ago and compulsive-obsessive patterns are
more frequent. Likewise, in both civilian and military life
cardiac symptoms have decreased in favor of gastrointestinal disturbances as reactions to severe stress (Grinker and
Spiegel, 1945). There has been a striking decrease of the
classical neuroses and a general increase in all forms of
overactive somatic disturbances associated with a change
in attitude toward the experience and expression of anxiety.
The role of the sick has under certain circumstances become sanctioned as an alternative to forbidden deviant or
delinquent behavior (Parsons, 1951). Defensive character
precipitates have, as a result, become much less severe or
less prematurely developed.

The core values of any society act upon the organism, to
the extent that its physical potentialities permit, within
phenotypes of mother-child relationship through what
Thompson (1951) has called the "psychosomatic set." The
two-way reaction between the cultural core value and the
"psychosomatic set" has been clearly indicated in the last
decade by scientific management of health problems on
Indian reservations in this country. Caudill has pointed out,
in his inventory of applications of anthropology to medicine, that culture cannot be considered as an outer layer

to be peeled off, leaving an inner layer that is noncultural (1953). The influence of culture is to be found in the content of every aspect of the psychosomatic organization, affecting its patterns as it matures and differentiates. Cultural influences are to be found in the content of the psychological id, the structure of the ego, and the forms of superego and ego-ideal. Culture determines the sanctioned characterological defenses, the unbearable precipitating crises culminating in illness, the type of illness, and the selective acceptance of social interactions in the therapeutic settings (Stanton and Schwartz, 1949). As Charles Johnson stated (1953), "The social sciences have furnished the foundation which enabled psychiatry to link medicine with the social situation within the broad control of culture." The modern psychosomatic approach has come to recognize that the functioning of every part of the organism is molded by the culture within which the individual has developed.

There are many valuable contributions to the field of psychosomatic medicine that have not been discussed. Many of them emphasize particular syndromes of somatic disorders as states of disordered physiology, others as reactions to specific life situations or occurring in special types of personality. A variety of measurements have been made, from enzymes to cortical electrical potentials. Some have delved deeply into unconscious processes in persons suffering from somatic disorders or in patients at the same time under experimentation through normal body openings or through those pathologically or surgically caused. However, the theoretical concepts of all these studies generally follow the positions of those workers whose ideas I have already outlined, so that further reference to them does not serve the purpose of this book.

It now seems appropriate to attempt an evaluation of the explicit theoretical formulations with a view to appraising their significance, adequacy, and relationship to basic empirical observations, and to evaluate their concomitant operational procedures.

CHAPTER FOUR

Evaluation of Theoretical Formulations and Operational Procedures

EVALUATION of the existing theoretical positions held by the chief investigative groups working in psychosomatic medicine becomes more difficult with the passage of time. From the later formulations of each there can be discerned an apparent trend toward agreement and a tolerant acceptance of pluralistic concepts of etiology and mechanism. Differences have been attributed to the methods of observation, oriented toward varying depths of psychological processes or greater details of physiological mechanisms. Contributions to the field emanating from all sorts of investigators, from psychoanalysts to enzyme chemists, are accepted without reference to a specific context within any theoretical scheme. At the same time each group goes on with its own methods, publishing more and more of the same kind of material, so that formulations have become repetitive, significant controversy has declined, and new concepts and methodologies have not been developing.

When we survey the existing theoretical formulations in terms of the distance of most observers from the objects of their study, their significance becomes clearer. Halliday observes nosological entities against the background of a sick society. Social anthropologists describe patterns of child raising as precursors to specific personality and character types against the background of different social and cultural groups. Ruesch analyzes disturbances of communication as indices of psychosomatic disorders against the background of development in early life. Wolff measures smooth-muscle function of organs and their blood vessels and of glands against the background of life situations. Dunbar studies personality behavior against the background of disease entities as items within medical nosological classification. Alexander describes personality in somewhat greater detail in varying states of self-reported and quantitatively estimated illness. All these observers are far removed from at least one of their objects, whether this is society or a physical complaint.

Considering the methods of observation, some investigators view a specific organ's changing functions, during spontaneously or experimentally induced life situations, in correlation with the concomitant emotional reactions experienced consciously and reported by the subject or interpreted from his behavior. The functional alterations in the organs observed are stereotyped, and variability exists only in the shifting site of the organic changes, although no observer has viewed any significant combination of organs to determine simultaneity or succession of activity, or a shifting interaction of innervation. Other investigators view some unconscious emotional processes, without going to the depths of the most significant experiences occurring at a preverbal age, during remissions and recrudescences of a specific disturbance under scrutiny. These disturbances are located at a site corresponding to the presenting complaint or dysfunction, and are often measured inadequately and too infrequently. Another group views the behavior patterns of individuals who suffer from a general organ-system disturbance as though it were a steady state. In such a procedure the organ dysfunction is accepted as a stereotype from the diagnosis, and the behavior patterns are reconstructed from the history of the patient and his relatives without the benefit of direct observation. Still other observers, who are more interested in the social aspects of the field, view the individual as a statistic, not identifiable as a person, living within a generalized, unmeasurable, descriptively defined social state.

The choice of correlations, or the figure and ground of the gestalt, of individual studies has not really been determined by theoretical assumptions. On the contrary, this choice is the result of the operational methods within the discipline in which each investigator has been trained and in which he feels most comfortable. The theoretical formulations have arisen secondarily and therefore do not give the researcher or his readers a sense of completeness or adequacy. This is inevitable from the very nature of the diverse subject matter of the multiple part-systems, sub-wholes, and wholes of living processes which require special techniques for investigation. What is criticizable, however, is the failure of the investigators, working especially with unitary comprehensive concepts called psychosomatic, to identify their positions and purposes as observers in relation to defined objects of study.

In any psychosomatic research in which the relationships of functions of parts to other parts, or parts to a whole, are under scrutiny, not only the identification of the observer's position in time and space, but also the identification of what is under observation is necessary. In many researches the latter is missing or, if present, inaccurate. If in a system of innumerable foci within the innervation of the vegetative nervous system, one such as the stomach is chosen, what psychological foci may be identified as corollary? In an analysis of a specific psychodynamic tendency, which visceral function should be identified as a corollary?

The methods of choice and identification of significant foci involved in co-relations must be carefully scrutinized. The technique of relying on the patient's specific complaint or the signal of distress that enters his consciousness, to the exclusion of all others, removes scientific control from the investigation. The use of a specific life situation or a report of a moment, hour, or day of dreams, thoughts, or behavior artificially restricts the psychological data. The quest for exact and accurate measurement of emotions, which are obtained only through some form of self-reporting, cannot be satisfied by analysis of the current life situations, unconscious defenses, or secondary affects alone. At present the methods that have been utilized have not accurately selected, or defined, focal process in space or time and have not reached the basic qualities of their functions, whether somatic or psychological, perhaps with the exception of Margolin *et al.* (1950), who psychoanalyzed to great depths a patient whose artificially exposed gastric mucosa was subjected to direct observation and experimentation.

Another major difficulty is concerned with time. Psychological and somatic observations are rarely made simultaneously, so that in at least one sphere past events must be reconstructed, or present activities attributed to initiation at another time. Latency of propagation, circular perpetuating processes initiated in past time, and feedback mechanisms detached from the original stimulus, are all factors that create difficulties when observations of interacting systems are not made simultaneously over reasonably long periods of time. The time element brings into consideration the difficulties in making valid statements concerning the development of somatic functions as foci within the total organismal system. Psychiatric investigations into psychosomatic problems usually utilize the techniques of psychoanalysis, and most current basic assumptions are derived from data based on reconstructions. How deep these analyses go—that is, how far they penetrate into past time and what somatic signals they use—is of utmost significance, yet these variables are rarely accounted for.

The utilization of several cross sections of transactional activity among somatic, psychic, and environmental systems at various times could give us a better idea of the longitudinal processes.

Rarely has the psychosomatic field been approached from the point of view that it is a field. Correlations have been made between certain somatic dysfunctions and supposedly connected, related, or correlated specific feelings, not as co-variables, but as effect and cause. Genetic or current concomitants in time, of psychological and somatic disturbances, are adopted as criteria of psychophysical unity, although most investigators tacitly deal with the concept of parallelism with occasional cross channels. Their work permits only a circumscribed view of the field which is much larger in time and space than each identifies. The inability of any one investigator to describe and measure more than a single aspect of the field, or for that matter to take a position at more than one point at a time, makes it necessary for him to work with other investigators. One observer describing a small sector of the field from an identifiable position can delineate the boundaries at which his operational methods cease to function, and relegate to another observer with other techniques the task of describing and measuring the changes in his system. Once an initial field approach to any situation is utilized and the system foci under observation are defined, all others should be identifiable as constant variables. However, since the psychosomatic-social field exists simultaneously in time, the most effective means of dealing with several systems in transaction is the utilization of multiple observers with different frames of reference measuring changes in activities *at the same time.*

The field concept will be discussed later, in Chapter X, but here it may be mentioned that multidisciplinary research should have been carried on in psychosomatic medicine for some time. However, psychoanalysts frequently object, because of a rigid "therapeutic attitude," to permitting their patients to be tested in laboratories while in treatment. Many seem to be unduly disturbed at the advent of somatic signals of distress (the "passagère symptom" of Ferenczi), which are most important as indirect evidences of significant somatic processes involved in some manner with the emotional problems under focus. On the other hand, physiologists and psychoanalysts often contend that multidisciplinary research is developmental, whereas creative research of a basic orientative nature is done by men working alone. This I believe to be partially the cause of lopsided psychosomatic correlations.

This brings us to the fact that psychosomatic research has been pioneered by medical men, often with traditional views concerning essential differences between health and disease. In a fine essay, George Engel (1953) discusses the unitary concept of health and disease: "Health represents the phase of successful adjustment, disease the phase of failure. When a stimulus is encountered the organism must deal with it, regardless of its source. If the capacity of the organism to deal with the stimulus is adequate, no disruption of equilibrium occurs and a state of health persists. If the stimulus cannot be dealt with, we recognize it as a stress which now upsets the previous homeostatic balance and disease is the consequence. If the stress is overwhelming the patient may die. Or a successful balance may again be achieved with no impairment of function, in which case health is restored, although the individual is no longer the same as before. Or a new balance may be achieved but at the price of considerable restriction of function."

Discrimination between the phases of health and illness as separate entities is now historical, yet many investigators still make this artificial and sharp distinction. It seems that psychosomatic correlations should be studied not only in individuals with seriously impaired function by observers with the "therapeutic urge," but also by analysis of stages of developing, and existing, well-balanced equilibrium. To overcome the many obstacles to research in psychosomatic medicine and to fulfill certain criteria of scientific evidence, it would seem that two general methodological principles should be employed. One is the study of the maturation and differentiation of psychosomatic processes (*genetic—* not exclusively psychogenic). The other is the use of multidisciplinary, simultaneous, prolonged observations of many phases of integration and disintegration of psychosomatic processes (*transactional*). Both of these will be discussed in detail in future chapters, but first I shall outline certain significant empirical observations.

CHAPTER FIVE

Empirical Observations

CONCERN with relations between emotional constellations and organ syndromes dominates much of contemporary psychosomatic investigation. Medical interest in the concept that special psychodynamic tendencies, through a chain of physiological events, could be at least partially responsible for dysfunction and morphological changes of specific organs, has delayed investigations into the primary psychosomatic processes. I believe that the central focus should not be either on the nature of the somatic functions, which is the subject matter of physiology, or on the psychological processes, which are independently studied by psychologists, psychiatrists, and psychoanalysts, but on the forces contributing to psychosomatic unity, its developmental differentiation, and its unhealthy disintegration.

At birth the infantile organism exists in its most complete state of extrauterine unification, undifferentiation, or wholeness. At that time the acceptance and significance of stimuli are difficult to detect, but on the effector side, the generalized nature of the infant's activities and reactions can be easily observed. In response to an internal need such as hunger or thirst, or in reaction to an external stimulus creating discomfort of any kind, such as heat, the child's total available motor and secretory functions seem to be activated. Within a few months, as it comes to recognize the meaningful and significant people in its environment, separation or rejection serves as a similar external stimulus in the psychological field. No matter whether the stimulus is internal or external, somatic or psychological, the child has a similar early pattern of total behavior in response to frustrations of its needs. It has a very low sensory threshold, lower than ever again in its life (Mirsky, 1953). It cries, salivates, regurgitates, and defecates; its face becomes red and vigorous random movements occur in muscles of the trunk and appendages. It functions with everything it has available, responding with a total pattern of integrated mass action. This generalized excitement is the child's first aggression—in the service of self-preservation.

We do not know the meaning of these various stimuli to the child except insofar as we are able to identify with or anthropomorphize the child's preverbal feelings. In fact, we do not know when the psychological system reaches that maturity which enables an imprint of meaning to become lasting. However, we can correlate the various reactions with their stimuli, categorize them as responses to disturbances of equilibrium, and establish their significance as *precursors* to fear and anger. Whatever the nature of the stress, the reaction to it is stereotyped and general, for all organ systems seem to participate with reactions of ejection, riddance, evasion, avoidance, or whatever terms various investigators have considered appropriate. There is little discrimination in time or quantity of response or part response to a stress situation.

Greenacre (1952), expresses the observations of total reaction in a different way. "If the traumata, distress or frustrations of the earliest months are particularly severe, the stimuli do not remain focused, but overflow through the body and act upon various organs." We see direct evidence of this in the oral, excretory, and genital responses at birth and during the stresses of earliest infancy. These responses may be activated simultaneously rather than in an orderly progression.

Benedek (1949), speaks of the "not yet quite organized vegetative nervous system," so that the first weeks of life are characterized by vegetative irritability. These are manifested in total responses including irregular respiration, sneezing, yawning, regurgitation, vomiting, fitful waking, startle response, etc. She states, "Since a psychic organization in which id is distinguished from ego emerges only gradually as a result of growth, from the point of view of personality organization the neonatal period represents an undifferentiated phase. The whole psychology of the newborn is in the service of survival alone." These total growth processes become a reservoir of energies which later differentiate as to quantity, direction, and aim.

Under certain circumstances the adult organism, which

has lost its diffuse or mass responses through processes of differentiation because of maturation, demonstrates their revival during regressive return to the primacy of total behavior. In anaphylactic shock Ryle (1939) has described the total vegetative response of diarrhea, urticaria, arthritis, asthenia, hypotension, etc., as a massive synchronous excitation of the vegetative nervous system. Greenacre, from the psychological studies of children, states in psychoanalytic terms that the early polymorphous discharge of tension leaves these channels always available for discharge in later life. Then, during periods of heightened anxiety, frustration, and danger, the flow of activity is conducted over old channels reviving the overflow responses of early life.

The last war taught us a great deal about the reactions of the mind and body under sudden and severe stress (Grinker and Spiegel, 1945). Severity of the stress was not the only important factor in the development of psychosomatic symptoms; qualitative factors of type of stress and degree of preparation were also significant. Those who had been free for years from previous symptoms redeveloped the same ones no matter what the stress. Actual observation indicated the universality of vomiting and diarrhea, headache, and tachycardia as substitute reactions to situations normally evoking fear, rage, and crying; and headache and tachycardia had the same emotional basis. Each symptom was the somatic expression of *several* emotions, and the *same emotions* could be found underlying a *variety*

of somatic expressions. The unconscious emotional processes accompanying acute psychosomatic symptoms were
complicated mixtures associated with conscious feelings,
thoughts, and verbalizations. More severe disturbances
demonstrated revivals of total patterns of infantile activity.
In such cases peripheral circulatory disturbances, crying,
vomiting, diarrhea, random inco-ordinated muscular movements, infantile postures, stuttering, etc., were examples of
mass responses of undifferentiated activities.

Psychosomatic syndromes are indications not only of
failure to attain, but also of a dissolution of, adult psychological organization—in other words, a regression to less
mature psychological adaptations or less mature phases of
growth or development. I use the word "adaptation" ad-
visedly, because during the war we observed that these
syndromes held back or delayed processes toward more
severe dissolutions of the personality. Likewise, in civilian
life ill-advised tampering with psychosomatic states sometimes results in more serious psychotic manias or depressions. Regression to visceral modes of expression seems to
be teleologically significant as a protective (flight) device
and to be of the same nature as regression to previously
present, but abandoned, patterns of behavior, such as stuttering, nail biting and enuresis. Such expressions may
represent not only a particular emotion or need, but also a
previously learned infantile technique of coping with an
overwhelming environmental stress that stimulates a host
of anxiety-producing internal reactions. Observe the child

and his near-conscious combating of hostile environmental forces by his choice of one or two symptoms of gagging, vomiting, headache, diarrhea, crying, enuresis, temper tantrums, bulimia, anorexia, etc., and the impotency of the adult world to deal with these reactions. It should not be surprising that several emotions may be expressed by the same peripheral visceral activity. The final common pathway of the nervous system, whether somatic or autonomic, discharges impulses from many private pathways in an identical manner. The autonomic nervous system especially reacts in response to overwhelming affective stimuli with a diffuse and almost mass discharge (Grinker, 1947).

Through the vagaries of life situations, or the accidents of special relationships, or the use of pharmacological or hormonal therapies such as cortisone, the personality structure may crumble and the psychosomatic syndrome is superseded by a psychotic breakdown. In such a breakdown the exposed psychodynamics and the type of psychosis are not differentiated or specific to any special type of psychosomatic disorder previously present.

A particular psychosomatic expression is not constantly related to a specific emotional constellation. Psychotherapy or psychoanalysis may shift the symptom from one system to another. It is a well-known observation that symptoms may vary spontaneously (crying-migraine, asthma-eczema). Kepecs, Robin, and Brunner (1951) have shown experimentally that in individuals free from skin disease increased transudation occurs through the skin when weeping is inhibited and the appropriate stimulus for weeping is suggested under hypnosis. Furthermore, when eczematous patients are given the suggestion to weep lacrimally, their normally weeping skin is less permeable for transudation. Thomas French (1941) reported that dreams indicate a shift of energy from organ to organ depending on the problem being solved and the method available at the time.

Kepecs (1953) noted the frequent shifting of somatic manifestations of emotional disturbances from one region or functional system of the body to another. These are the product of the interaction of three factors: the psychological significance of the shift, the psychological significance of the organs or region involved, and the anatomic and physiologic properties of the organs or regions utilized. Such a complicated interaction deals with more than simple involvement of organs normally stimulated concomitantly by a particular emotion, and indicates permutations which can only be analyzed in terms of general psychological and physiological functions plus personal experiences.

Felix Deutsch's (1949, 1950, 1951, 1952) modern psychosomatic concepts indicate that he conceives of functions, symptoms, and posture less as expressive symbols and more as means of discharge of physiological energy: "If a psychic stimulus presses for discharge the functional organic process initiated by the stimulus—a muscular movement for example, which leads to a postural rearrangement—continues and completes the psychological." Motivations causing movements of the voluntary musculature are inseparably intermingled with unconscious autonomic innervations. Furthermore, the invisible bodily behavior is integrated into the psychosomatic pattern just as is the visible, and is a result of experiences during the biological and psychological development which become part of the behavior pattern. From this and other evidence it may be stated that fragmented activity associated with emotional tension occurs in structures innervated by both vegetative and voluntary nervous systems without sharp separation.

Wolff (1950) states that in all psychosomatic disturbances induced by life situations the disordered physiological concomitants of affects are in the nature of hypersecretion, hyperemia, and hypermotility. I would assume that the hypersecretion or increase in free fluid may be a primary and fundamental physiological process accompanying the psychological state of primary dependency. As the ego boundaries diminish in a severely regressive state, the permeability of cellular membranes increases, a correlation which may stimulate speculation regarding primitive ways of maintaining homeostatic balance as contrasted with more developed and evolved humoral and neural methods.

Such observations as I have selectively cited seem to indicate that primary vegetative reactions to stress or need are undifferentiated, that severe regressive modes of response to catastrophic stress in adult life repeat the early infantile pattern, and that when discrete fragments of this global response are present, they occur within systems (not specific to organs or disease) and are interchangeable under

certain circumstances. Furthermore, both the basic psychodynamics and physiodynamics of different fragmentary
visceral dysfunctions are more alike than dissimilar, both
representing "final common pathways." These observations
naturally stimulate our interest in the origin of the fragments of the total pattern and how the parts are linked to
the whole.

CHAPTER SIX

Psychosomatic Differentiation

THE HUMAN infantile organism, on becoming detached from its mother, is born with certain built-in hereditary, functional patterns which are innate to its structures and are part of its phylogenetic inheritance. Some differences or variations may be genotypic and constitutional; others have occurred in the numerous processes of intrauterine development. Many differences arise from prenatal influences dependent upon the mother's physical and emotional health and behavior, and the duration and vicissitudes of passage through the birth canal. Freud (1936) and lately Greenacre (1945) have speculated on the influences of the processes of birth and of the first impinging stimuli on the later development of the child, but at the present time we can only place all these prenatal and birth experiences in a single category of variables, yet to be studied and evaluated.

At first the embryonic organism acts on its environment through its intrinsic patterns of functions, since its sensory and perceptive systems have not developed. They come into action later and only then permit the organism to respond in reaction to its environment. As an undifferentiated whole, committed only to those structuralized functions that are species-bound, the infant has his highest degree of potentiality, but also his highest degree of sensitivity, because stimuli impinging on him early lastingly affect all of him, no matter how much differentiation later occurs. A homologue in embryology is the effect of trauma on multi-potential embryonic tissue whose later differentiating parts carry a lasting imprint in their subsequent organization. Later traumatic events acting on a more organized somatic or psychologic structure or function are limited in site and localization of effect.

The infant's first responses show very little variation in type from individual to individual. They occur when a threshold level is reached, which is usually low, but depends upon the general reservoir of available energy, the degree of sensitivity, and the extent of the possible responsiveness, all of which characterize innate irritability (cf. Chapter XI). At birth infants may be grossly categorized as to their rapidity of reaction to the environment and the quantity of motor or secretory activity within such response. There are good babies who never whimper, incessantly crying babies, babies who never seem hungry, and others who are aggressively hungry.

The responsiveness of the infant at birth is unconditioned and general within the limits of his species' capacity to action. Coghill (cf. Herrick, 1949), clearly demonstrated that in amblystoma total swimming movements first appear, and that when stimulated the larval organism always responds with the same type of general movements, out of which differentiation develops. Such differentiation is in the nature of individual reflex activity through functions of parts of those structures which were originally involved in the total movement patterns. The individuation or differentiation of movements utilizes part of what was present at birth in mass action. In all species the form of differentiation is limited by their available organization, but learning also influences the extent and content of such differentiation (cf. Corner, 1944).

In spite of such differentiation the total pattern is never lost, because under certain circumstances it may again assume dominance. The asynchronous activities of individual processes may be again superseded by a synchronous coordinated total pattern. In fact, Coghill stated that the part derived from the whole at first is in functional conflict with the whole for dominance. Conflict and rivalry among parts results in shifting inhibitions which are the matrix of the novel and out of which problem solving, learning, and intelligent behavior arise. In fact, this applies as high as the level of consciousness, for that component of behavior only arises from "long circuiting" when unconscious lower-level adjustments are inadequate. This is a precursor of Launcelot Whyte's (1948) statement, "Thought is born of failure. When action satisfies there is no residue to hold the attention: To think is to express a lack of adjustment which we must stop to consider. Only when the human organism fails to achieve an adequate response to its situation is there material for the processes of thought and the greater the failure the more searching they become." In Freud's terms thinking is trial action.

Coghill's finding that primary mass action preceded individuation and differentiation did not assume that spontaneous action is uncaused, but predicated activity of living, equilibrated, open systems disturbed first by inherent internal rhythms and later by external influences. The organism tends to maintain its integrity while independencies develop within it. These common intrinsic forces one may call instinctive, before the period of primitive awareness of external stimuli. Novel and creative patterns are determined by dynamic responses to later external influences—the first learning process. Any theory of motivation must, therefore, be based upon a consideration of intrinsic sources of energy and action.

However, the primary quality of elementary awareness of internal need and satiation or external change is a phenomenon that is genetic to consciousness and feelings, which are functions of the whole organism. Mentation is present in behavior at all levels as integrated action based on phylogenetic and ontogenetic past, projected into the future for purposes of survival, and is, therefore, a merging of past and future with the present (see also Bentley, 1950). Thus, Coghill considers mentation as part of the total pattern of action and reaction, out of which elaboration of complicated psychological functions occurs. Later, each part function does not struggle to maintain its supremacy over other parts and against the whole; rather, an orderly integration develops among the differentiated patterns with determinant functions which defend against disintegration. The embryogenesis of differentiation of part patterns and their integration to form a new whole is an important concept not only in embryology, but also in psychiatry and psychosomatic medicine.

Probably nowhere is this process of differentiation and reintegration more clearly expressed in a psychological sense than in some of Freud's early formulations of zones of libidinal organization. Later Freud considered mass or total actions in the newborn infant as lack of "Reitzschutz," and at the same time he postulated several levels of expression of psychic energy. These depended upon the development and readiness of a hierarchy of organs, all of them eventually relinquishing their roles to become part of a new whole—the mature, integrated, and genital adult. Contrast this with Alexander's overflow or surplus-energy theory of mature giving and genitality.* In my opinion mature integration can never be considered as "surplus." Should development not proceed normally, fixation at one or more levels occurs. Under certain conditions, disintegration of the whole is associated with regression to more infantile or primitive levels, or still further to the less dif-

* Separation from the child-mother symbiosis and development begins with the maturation of the great sensory systems and the central reticular structures, and the capacity to store energy-producing substances.

ferentiated psychotic state. Out of the total pattern, independent part activities develop with spontaneity, autonomy, and initiative, and varying rise and fall of dominance, always utilizing part of the total pattern and always capable of relinquishing autonomy to fall back into the old synchronous mass action.

Schneider (1949), following Coghill's work, has also considered that growth and maturation of ideas and feelings occurs by differentiation from an undifferentiated pattern. After the initial effects of anxiety and the forces of growth impinge on the developing brain, disturbing its "tension-relaxation equilibrium," conditioned reflexes and idea-feeling patterns develop. They become organized and are no longer easily affected by growth or anxiety to produce basically new ideas or new reflexes. Ideas and feelings cannot at full growth be directly correlated with somatic processes because the fully developed "tension-equilibrium" system is an end result into which the forces of growth have expended themselves. However, I do not consider that any differentiated system can be so completely specialized and detached that it cannot be influenced to some degree by progressive or regressive changes in other parts of the whole.

In his discussion of psychoanalytic concepts and specifically of the theory of affects, Rapaport (1951) uses an ontogenetic model that indicates increasing complexity with development. The primary model of psychic processes begins with the restless hunger of the infant demanding, and receiving, gratification resulting in quiescence. The rest-lessness is the first expression of an affect charge, to which, and to the gratification of which, become attached memory traces. "Affects use—to begin with—inborn channels and thresholds of discharge. These may be considered appa-ratuses pre-existing the differentiation of ego and id from their undifferentiated matrix. In this respect affects are common properties of the species, and this may have to do with the roots of their social role in communication and empathy. Yet even in this respect there are already at birth great inter-individual differences which have to do with what develops into predisposition to anxiety and into various affect-equivalents in psychosomatic pathology . . ." (1952).

Hartmann (1951) has re-emphasized Freud's discussion of primal congenital ego variations, indicating that hereditary factors partake in the determination of the development, tendencies, and reactions of the ego. Hartmann uses the principle of maturation by differentiation when he states: "I should rather say that both the ego and the id have developed, as products of differentiation, out of the matrix of animal instincts." Thus, the human id estranged from reality is a differentiation and not a direct continuation of animal instincts (Piaget's "undifferentiated absolute," 1930). The final step in differentiation occurs in the con-flictless sphere of the ego which Hartmann terms the autonomous ego. The ego in its own right ultimately becomes a pattern which functions with desexualized and disaggressivized energy.

In the processes of development and differentiation of the psychological system, symbolic-meaning patterns become a constituted part of the human personality. These are often described as psychological "structures" or "organs" instead of functions. Psychoanalysts use terms such as "the ego," "the superego," or "the ego-ideal." These functions as part of and constituting personalities enable people to interact by means of several, often rapidly changing, roles, thereby constituting a social system. Institutionalization of varieties of social roles constitutes patterns of culture (Parsons, 1953).

Thus, from the first generalized, undifferentiated behavior of the newborn, differentiation, reintegration, and the development of systems of functional patterns have culminated in symbolic processes which are basic to the development of personality and of social and cultural systems. Each is dependent upon biological, social, and cultural processes in its evolution and differentiation, after which each system, although in transaction with the others and a constituent of the whole, progresses within and to its own limitations.

Physiological embryologists have demonstrated that the earliest stimuli or stresses impinging on the maturing embryo affect all its parts which differentiate from the whole. Stone (1938) suggests that early psychic influences affecting an individual also have a greater tendency to produce generalized chronic, overt, or latent disturbances in growth, metabolism, and visceral functions. Later traumata acting at special periods of localized heightened growth activities may result in specific damage and reactions. Michaels (1944, 1945) points out that psychosomatic disturbances in adults resemble the "hyperfunctioning" of the vegetative nervous system of infants in its abrupt changes, wide homeostatic range, high degree of lability, and greater cellular permeability. Michaels describes the organ dysfunction of enuresis accompanying psychopathic disturbances and states that these are two aspects (psychosomatic) derived from early predisposition and experiences affecting the whole personality (1941).

Differentiation and development of specialized functions within parts of the whole which in itself matures, expands, and evolves, creates the need for more complicated patterns of integration. Communication of parts in juxtaposition or bathed by the same fluids, circulating humoral processes and more complicated neural pathways constitute varying levels of complexity in integration. To paraphrase Hughlings Jackson (1886), integration is represented and re-represented from the level of cellular proximity to the highest level of association fibers within the cerebral cortex. Integration is effected by methods as simple as chemical osmosis or electrical conduction across a cellular membrane or as complicated as the highest level of association of symbols.

Neurophysiological findings and theories during the last twenty years have contributed a great deal to the understanding of visceral and psychological differentiation and their re-integration at higher levels. Earlier work (Papez, 1937; Grinker, 1939b, etc.) emphasized the role of the diencephalon in its effector functions of emotional expression through visceral innervations and the phasic two-way relations between cerebral cortex and diencephalon. More recent work (Brodal, 1947; MacLean, 1949; Penfield, 1951; Kuntz, 1951; etc.) suggests that the limbic cortical structures, rather than olfactory in nature, should be considered as constituting the visceral brain. These structures are concerned with integration of feeling-needs and deal with information crudely transformed into language derived from enteroceptive material, corresponding to the organ language of the primitive, infantile, dependent or oral state of patients with psychosomatic disturbances and infants in the first three months of life. Kubie (1953a) speculates that the visceral brain is activated from the central reticular substance and is the association area of communication between internal and external perceptions. It deals with impressions of past and present, inside and outside, and is concerned in the synthesis and elaboration of impulses basic for the neocortex in its formation of word symbols. Thus, every symbolic unit represents simultaneously internal and external experiences obtained through proprioceptive and exteroceptive sense organs. If one aspect of such representation is lost, psychopathology develops of varying type depending on which aspect is disturbed.

Kubie, considering that each symbol has a bipolarity—external and internal—believes that verbal memories constitute a screen which hides gut memories as intellectualizations hide insight. For a process of reliving and subsequent re-orientation there must be a somatic participation with a breakdown of the boundaries between past and present in order to insure the revival of such gut memories (see also Margolin's anaclitic therapy on page 87). "Thus it is through the temporal lobe and the visceral brain that the 'gut' component of memory can enter into our psychological processes; and it is precisely here that the multipolar areas of reference of the symbolic function can be served. Consequently, we are justified in saying that the temporal lobe, with its deeper primitive connections, is a mechanism for the coordination of all the data which link us to the world of experience, both external and internal. It is through these mechanisms that we are able to project and introject; and it is through these central structures which serve the multipolarity of symbolic function that the central nervous organ can mediate the translation into somatic disturbance of those tensions which are generated on the level of psychological experience. It is this area of the brain then which deserves to be viewed as the organ which is essential for psychosomatic relationships."

Clinical neurology based on Jacksonian postulates also deals with the differentiation of new functions, which become integrated into the total organization by damping down functions of the older structures of the nervous system. These become released and revived after damage to their inhibitors (Grinker, 1939a). It is well known, furthermore, that the body image or somatic ego develops before and after birth by successive steps in differentiation. Successive phases in development of the body image become prominent and are then superseded by more mature forms; but they never disappear, for they can be revived under the influence of strong emotion. This also holds true in the development of language (Cooper, 1952).

It seems clear that aside from the primitive needs of open systems to maintain equilibrium with their environments and an internal homeostasis, there is an expansive trend toward differentiation, growth, and learning in the individual, and emergent evolution of the species. Life in individuals and species is restless, expansive, progressive, and changing to form new stable systems. For the individual the crucial pathogenic period lies in that stage at which total functions are giving way in growth to individuation with attendant new forms of integration. We shall now turn to an examination of this stage in the maturing human infant.

CHAPTER SEVEN

Factors Influencing Psychosomatic Differentiation in Health and Illness

SINCE health and illness constitute a continuum rather than sharply differentiated categories, their development follows similar patterns of transaction between organism and environment, each of which has the possibility of an infinite number of variabilities. Our first important question concerns the possible methods of observation, isolation, and interpretation of these variables in development, and their evaluation in terms of the end results in more or less healthy psychosomatic integrations.

The method of psychoanalysis of adults has opened broad fields for the investigation of phases of psychosomatic development. The reconstructed data from psychoanalysis of adults have lately been studied for the possibility of determining preverbal processes, but the earliest crucial periods are hardly ever reached. Conclusions from current transference feelings, intense though they may be, are only faint shadows on the present of what was once a bright light in the past. Reconstructed analyses are particularly unsuited for investigations into primary psychosomatic processes, especially since many analysts are willing to accept secondary character defenses as the significant primary derivatives of infantile feelings. Psychoanalytic investigations of children reveal much, but not enough, of current child-mother relationships, and early experiences are delineated even less clearly than with data obtained from adults. However, from psychoanalyses of both adults and children much valuable information has been obtained as to the effect of external stresses and deprivations, at various times, upon various modes of adaptation.

Child observations have been exploited in the last several decades in a systematic manner which Gesell and Armatruda (1941) call a "psychomorphological" approach. Their work concerns the unfolding of a patterned or ontogenetic behavior, which is built in as a species inheritance, through time sequences of growth relations. This presumes that the embryogenesis of mind is to be found in the development of postural behavior as well as vision (Gesell and Ilg, 1939) and neglects most of the interactions between child and mother, and other aspects of the environment.

Although most psychoanalysts (Fries, 1944) are dissatisfied with child-mother observations and contend that they must enter into a transference relationship with one of the symbiotic members in order to discern feeling reactions, Spitz (1947) has faithfully described and recorded the developing and changing child-mother unit. He has classified various effects of disturbances in this unit as "psychotoxic" diseases, each one correlated with a specific maternal attitude or deficit. Spitz (1950) concludes that infantile learning is divided into two phases. In the first phase excitation is superseded by quiescence on appropriate gratification, which produces primitive learning by conditioning. The second phase is one in which feelings of pleasure and unpleasure dominate, as the learning process becomes more human and is achieved through forces of cathexis and development of memory traces. Such a dichotomy is probably not justified by time or dynamics (cf. page 126).

Each of the methods of investigation—psychoanalysis of adults, psychoanalysis of children, and child observation—apparently cannot stand alone. Nor is the picture completed by the study of non-literate cultures in an attempt to correlate character and psychosomatic types with variations of culturally imposed habits of feeding and elimination (Mead, 1949). All these methods are necessary. Yet even the combination requires sharp hypotheses, and observational techniques directed toward the crucial processes of psychosomatic differentiation and integration. Emphasis on maturation of voluntary muscular control, zones of incorporation and elimination, traumata, defenses, etc., although contributing much toward understanding psychological processes, misses these points of interest.

Since the work of Freud which called attention to the various *zones* which differentiate and play a part in libidinal satisfaction of the growing child, the almost exclusive attention of psychoanalysts has been directed toward their unfolding into what may be called psychological *modes* of dealing with interpersonal relationships (Rank, Putnam, and Rachlin, 1948). For example, Erikson (1950) has drawn elaborate diagrams showing how these zones become motor forces in interpersonal relationships and calls attention to the fact that mutual regulation between the child and the mother, as these zones are developing, determines to a large extent the modes of dealing with subsequent life situations. The child's desire and the mother's giving, the child's rage and frustration and the mother's punitive attitude, form the primary psychological gestalts of relations with and mastery of the environment.

Greenacre (1952) points out in a general conceptual scheme, also concerned with zones, that the earlier in life traumatic events occur, the greater their effect on the emotional sphere and the more their memories are somatized. Severe or prolonged trauma produces an intense impact, activating all available channels for the expression of the resultant excitement. Premature activation of libidinal zones results in the utilization of all channels of discharge, including those not ready. She emphasizes that the nature, extent, and timing of trauma influence the modal organization of the final character structure, as viewed from the technique of handling the oedipus complex and other interpersonal problems. Here the Freudian concept of critical vulnerability is highlighted in terms of actual trauma in early childhood. It has been pointed out that

forced feeding, early enemas, excessive cleanliness, and excessive or early training in gymnastic skills have a profound
effect on the developing neuromuscular mechanism, which
may later break down. Many children are robbed of infancy or the chance for spontaneous differentiation by
stimulation of precocity. The changing patterns of child
care seem not only to place a burden on the mother, but
also to prevent the demarcation of zonal differentiation.

Margolin (1953) also holds fast to the zonal concept of
differentiation, but in a somewhat broader context. The
maturing infant in the so-called oral stage of development
has a wide range of homeostatic fluctuation with reversibility and a low threshold of responsiveness. At first external
persons regulate the environment because of the child's
deficiency in homeostasis. The child's alarm is the cry to
which the environment responds as part of the child's body
regulatory devices: thus environment becomes part of the
first body ego. Later, the infant's own regulatory devices
take over and eventually, as its cortical centers mature, it
grows from an involuntary decorticate animal to one with
the capacity to delay gratification and to control its sensorimotor transactions with the environment. Referring to the
stages of maturation according to Freudian classification,
Margolin considers that the oral phase is associated with
the highest degree of tissue pathology and psychotic sub-
strate, the anal less and the genital least. Specificity of
reaction to stress increases with the maturity at which the
pattern of reaction to stress develops. Thus, Margolin

postulates variations in body-mind continuum (psychosomatic regulatory states in service of homeostasis and mastery of environment) from an undifferentiated, involuntary, oral phase to a differentiated, voluntary, centrally regulated, genital phase—each with its appropriate tolerances and reactions to stress.

In another context—one dealing with a therapeutic procedure termed "anaclitic"—Margolin considers psychosomatic disturbances in relation to feelings originating during preverbal stages of development. He considers psychosomatic disturbances as closely related to psychoses, often alternating with them spontaneously or as a result of ill-advised psychotherapy or hormonal therapy. Persons with psychosomatic disturbances tend to show regressive trends and have a restricted capacity for transference relationships. Margolin's goal in "anaclitic" therapy is to induce a physiological change and a remission of the disease. This he attempts by urging and facilitating, through intense mothering, a regression to infantile dependency, during which all the patient's wishes (particularly oral) within the realm of his experience are gratified, without his request and before his conscious knowledge of these needs. This is achieved through interpretation of the patient's nonverbal behavior, which serves as an analyzable synthetic dream. This gratification of needs and wishes anterior to the conflict period increases the patient's regressions, betters his mood, and decreases his somatic symptoms. During this process it may be assumed that an unconscious, pre-verbal, visceral relearning occurs. Following this procedure, weaning by means of verbal interpretations is attempted, to reverse the regression and reconstitute the ego's boundaries. Many doubts and controversies have arisen in discussions of Margolin's therapy, and results have not yet been reported, but the essential assumption behind this work seems to be correct. This states that psychosomatic disorders antedate verbalizations, defenses, higher levels of awareness, etc., and can be correlated only with needs and stresses which have impinged on the organism in its preverbal stage of development. Also psychosomatic disturbances are allied to preverbal feeling states which have lost, or have never achieved, their connections with word symbols referable to "not I" and can only be communicated at a visceral (feeling or mood) level (cf. also Ruesch).

Kubie (1948), in speculating on the internal somatic operations, relates them to the theory of instincts. These, he states, have an inherited nucleus and consist of three components—i.e., biochemical, inherited modifiable neuronal nets, and the psychic superstructure. The modifiable net is subject to maturation and development through experience and learning, and the links from tissue changes to neuromuscular responses may be inherited or learned through conditioning. But these links are, according to Kubie, not psychologically represented, and he quotes Sherrington (1941) as stating: "When the integrated individual can do nothing about it, mind forsakes the act." On the intaking side dependence is on the mother for food and water; on the output side there is no dependence, but interference feeds back an effect on the primary energy system of the instincts. Kubie accepts a learning capacity of the neuronal net but denies psychological representation except through the orificial vectors.

More recently (1953a) Kubie has decried the tendency to ascribe etiology of neurotic and psychosomatic disorders to the symptoms themselves or to the consequent difficulty they cause in interpersonal relations, object relations, and reality testing. He would search for some specific central deformation. He raises several important questions. Where is the human psychic apparatus most vulnerable in a specifically human way? How is vulnerability manifested? What kinds of distortion can result? Do differences serve to contrast normality, psychoses, and neuroses? Kubie immediately turns to the ego function of symbolization or the symbolic process, and states that human psychopathology arises as a distortion of the symbolic process and cannot occur in animals without this or in humans before it develops. There can be no infantile primal depression or psychosis, and Spitz's mother-child separation cannot cause a disease. Thus Kubie consistently searches for vulnerability at ever higher neuronal levels at which differentiation and integration are, as I have suggested before, re-represented.

In my opinion the central core of the psychosomatic problem is the period of differentiation from total hereditary to individual learned patterns and their integration into a new personal system. Any hypothesis concerned with psychosomatic functions or pathology should deal with the intermediate stage of development between the undifferentiated whole functional pattern and the integrated matured process. It is this period that determines the formation of a healthy, sick, or potentially sick organism.

Most previous investigations have dealt with the unfolding of spontaneously developing differentiated patterns as though they occurred in a vacuum, or have been limited to the study of techniques by which the human environment has handled a certain few of the child's budding potentialities. For the most part these have included motor functions and intaking and eliminative processes. Completely mysterious, unobserved, and unmeasured are the happenings in the vast area of the "in-between" carried on by many organs and organ systems innervated by the vegetative nervous system. In Carmichael's comprehensive *Manual of Child Psychology* (1946), for example, there are few evidences that psychological interest has centered on observations of variants of visceral behavior except as they deal with the zones of incorporation and elimination.

A variant of constitutional visceral function has recently been studied by Mirsky (1953). Pepsinogen is elevated in persons suffering from peptic ulcer, often before the development of the ulcer. A significant number of neonates show this same high quantity of pepsinogen. Such a child is destined to remain hungry and dependent on the mother, whose integrative capacity becomes strained, resulting in her "feeding back" rejection or hostility to the child. Thus a constitutional factor is responsible both for the development of gastric symptoms or ulcer and for a dependent or "oral demanding" personality type. Mirsky also points out the many permutations of mother-child transactions due to the varieties of sensory thresholds and integrations of the child and the variations in integrative capacities of the mother. The result could be a spectrum of psychosomatic patterns based on internal constitutional factors.

There has been little emphasis on the timing of development and on the relationship among the individual portions of the visceral nervous system. Concomitance, co-ordination, reciprocal inhibition, and temporal succession develop within the matrix of diffuse vegetative responses. Many smaller systems become specifically linked to each other through circular processes as a result of natural maturation plus special environmental influences which affect not only physiological processes but also psychological patterns developing at the same time. The hypothesis may be stated that visceral activity is subject to a learning or experiential process which, if it impinges upon the undifferentiated organism, influences differentiation and all systems subsequently differentiated, including the psychological.

What early experiences which impinge upon the child help to create individual differences? Variations of patterns within the infant at birth are numerous, but even these are due to more than hereditary destiny. Already cultural attitudes have influenced the child during gestation by prescribing degrees of activity of the mother, her diet, the type of clothes she wears, etc. During birth such factors as anesthesia, use of forceps, speed of resuscitation, are influences which act upon the child. Then almost at once the degree of isolation from the mother, the sterility of the nursery, the absence of early postnatal feeding, circumcision, etc., are among the variables of early environmental influences.

Sometimes these influences occur accidentally through serious or prolonged dysfunction as a result of microbic invasion or early enzymatic deficiency. Illness or deficiency within the infant not only affects it directly, but has an effect upon the mother which reverberates back to the child. Often this reaches a point at which persistent parasitic dependency for some functions is characterized by the term "secondary gain." Therese Benedek (1949) indicates how the child incorporates the emotional attitudes and anxieties of the mother. She states: "The psychodynamics of symbiosis is interrupted at birth but remains a functioning force directing and motivating mental and somatic interaction between mother and child." The needs of the mother may be expressed in a demand that the child remain dependent and sick (Sperling, 1949). Children often lose their psychosomatic symptoms on being removed from home. These are, however, gross interaction systems which occur accidentally during and following an illness.

More significant and universal is the effect which mother and her surrogates have on specific conditioned responses. These reflect personal emotional attitudes as developed in her by her own specific past development, the special values of the ethnic group from which she stems, or the general prevailing cultural milieu in which mother and child co-exist. These attitudes influence the unfolding differentiation within the psychosomatic matrix and are intimately bound to values. Some functions have high or positive values and are sought or encouraged, some have negative values and are discouraged or prohibited, others are permitted or tolerated in a neutral manner. Furthermore, timing is of great significance in the application of such values.

If the visceral mass-responses are permitted and accepted as healthy and expected reactions until the child begins to indicate readiness for differentiation and control, these will occur without loss. Development can occur without deficit and each part can persist as silent, utilitarian, and adequate responses. On the other hand, when fragments of the total adaptive pattern are prohibited too early, before they can be conditioned into appropriate responses, lacunae will appear in the subsequent integration. Rushing the infant in his development through the demand for control, anxious suppression of adaptive responses to intercurrent illness by attitude or medication, may obliterate important psychosomatic functions. An example may be given of the modern tendency of pediatricians to give universally, for febrile conditions of infancy, large and repeated doses of antibiotics before making an accurate diagnosis and without permitting the biological defense processes to operate. Immunity to many organisms does not have a chance to develop, and the individual remains dependent upon external factors in adjustment. Immune bodies are closely linked in their production and effects to a host of other biochemical processes, so that it may be hypothesized that considerable deficiency in many functions is the result. Other influences exerted by the mother and her contemporary culture on internal processes through diets, medications, vaccines, serums, laxatives, have a profound effect not only upon the orifices or gastrointestinal tract, but upon the entire vegetative net. As a result, adaptive development, responses to stress or expressions of anxiety, may be borne by other segments of the visceral pattern. Not only will there be relative absence of some functions or communications, but an overloading on others. When it is their turn to undergo modification or control by conditioning, more intense or prolonged training becomes necessary.

Anxiety, no matter what its source, in an adult activates certain visceral patterns which are specific to the individual no matter what the stress, in that each one has his particular way of feeling anxious. Some variations include sinking abdominal sensations, diarrhea, vomiting, dyspnea, sensation of lump in the throat, etc. Out of the generalized infantile expression of anxiety each person seems to have been conditioned to certain fragmentary visceral patterns, which were once functionally adaptive to some specific stress as the physiological expression of the homeostatic disturbance, but which have become accurate and faithful signals to the ego of all intrapsychic dangers. If the anxiety signal is intensified for any reason in anyone, more previously silent fragments appear until the old non-specific infantile pattern is reviewed in its entirety under conditions of panic or catastrophe. Thus, here too a selective differentiation has occurred in development through some form of conditioning. Under severe stress the conditioned reflexes disappear and diffuse irradiation of excitation reappears.

Many other examples of visceral functions which are modified by external factors acting at various times may be given. From the day of intrauterine viability to an indefinite endpoint, a multiplicity of environmental, social, and culturally derived orientations act on the infant. These variables with their infinite permutations can help us understand the psychosomatic processes if they can be classified into categories according to methods of application to the child, immediate effects, and their overt specific and latent long-term results. What are the operational procedures by which the mother-figure can influence the differentiating visceral pattern aside from dealing with intaking and eliminative functions, or by intensifying motor control in degree or by its premature application? If we were satisfied with these influences we would be content with the zonal and vector categories of Freud and Alexander respectively, but neither of these can account for the internal or "in-between" processes. This is truly a vast area of neglected research for which, however, I believe observations, experimentation, and measurements are possible. The wide acceptance of "well-baby" clinics offers an opportunity for long-term developmental studies of many processes of internal enzymatic, hormonal, immunological and metabolic functions, correlated with maternal influences at various time periods.

Let us now turn to a discussion of psychological derivatives of the primal psychosomatic organization and postulate what variations of function may be expected from early impressions at the period of differentiation. I believe that these may be considered in at least two large categories. One includes the effect on the rudimentary psychological system which is destined for differentiation and later maturation of its own functions. In the early period, influences on the growing organism may not have direct effects which can be observed by psychological techniques or expressed in psychological content. Rather, there is an influence on patterning of function which can be understood as a process without reference to content. Although we have had no experience as yet in studying the minor patterns so differentiated and have only been able to recognize generalities such as greed, satiation, hunger, there is a vast material that can be studied by existing methods. I have reference to subjects who suffer from severe somatic illness in early life who seem to have completely recovered as far as their organ functions are concerned. With full knowledge of the early somatic disorder, observations may be made on the psychological pattern to determine the permanent residues within that organization.

There exists a clinical entity called celiac syndrome, which is worthy of intensive study for what can be learned about the relations between somatic and psychological processes. I have worked with a patient who had suffered from this disease for the first eight years of his life, and who came to me after he developed incapacitating neurotic symptoms at the age of seventeen. Data pertinent to the concept of early influences impinging on the total organism and persisting in its differentiated parts will be mentioned briefly.

Celiac syndrome manifests itself shortly after birth as a disturbance in food assimilation due to the constitutional absence of the necessary digestive enzymes. The infant becomes emaciated and bloated, suffers severe pain from cramps, and has an almost continuous diarrhea with dehydration. Nevertheless, if an infant with celiac syndrome can be kept alive, between the ages of six and eight years pancreatic function or some compensatory activity develops so that the deficiency disappears, fats become digestible, and physical symptoms disappear. Such was the case in my patient, who recovered from his almost complete invalidism at about eight years of age. Diarrhea recurred only when fat digestion became greatly overloaded.

During the course of therapy it became apparent that the patient's mental operations were patterned almost exactly as his physical functions had been in the early years. His hungry yearning for mother's love was offset by the fear that she would poison him, for it was her administration of the food that gave him so much distress. His incapacity for enduring tension and his need for exact scheduling were counterparts of uncontrollable diarrhea and dietary regimes. In times of anxiety he would reproduce physical distension, and defenses against unpalatable interpretations included immediate fecal evacuation. All these methods were used for masochistic gratification. He would become hungry for knowledge and anticipate with a great deal of eagerness the possibility of studying a certain subject and mastering it next week. When the time came for his planned and scheduled learning process he devoured the material rapidly. He mulled over it in great preoccupation with detail and had the greatest difficulty in digesting the basic facts. Subsequently he would feel extremely tense and anxious unless he were able to explain what he had learned to other people, which he did repetitively over and over again, exploding with impatience when people did not understand him. After this bout he usually developed an empty feeling and became hungry and jealous, envious of other people who were able to continue school and learn at a regular rate. From this brief description one can see that a permanent effect of the lack of a proper digestive enzyme had been left on his psychological system long after it had differentiated and developed within its sphere apart from intestinal functions. When his organs functioned normally, digestive troubles subsided, but psychological activities remained in the same patterning as when he had the syndrome.

Such a constitutional process as celiac syndrome is revealed by grossly demonstrable disturbances in function. There are many important constitutional differences in biochemical processes that are not clear, yet influence the child's needs and demands. Grinker, Ham, and Robbins (1950) hypothesized in multiple sclerosis that "in some children there is a greater constitutional need and hence a greater dependency on external dietary sources of supply through which chemical and physiological integration may be achieved and emotional maturity apparently reached." The greater demands subtly made by such children tax the capacity of the human environment and frustration ensues, or the acquiescence of the mother figure may be at the expense of greater demands by her on the child. Such transactional processes should be viewed from the frame of reference of child or mother as arcs of a cycle changing, often *spirally*, in time and ultimately taxing one of the organisms beyond its capacity to maintain its own integration. Thus constitutional differences are precursors to a continually changing transacting process which cannot be described adequately as "fixation." Labeling of the child as a congenital or constitutionally inadequate organism or of the mother as a punitive, cold, unloving, rejecting figure does not help our understanding of the total process.

Benedek (1953) has stressed a field concept of intrapsychic forces in the development and functions of the ego, which constitutes a method of considering the influence of early total experiences on personality. She states that early stress, when it endangers survival at the time of greatest ego weakness, stimulates adaptation of the instinctual forces to effect a change, often radical. These vicissitudes of the instincts reduce their subsequent adaptability in that they become grooved in their expressions and somewhat rigid or restricted into personality patterns. Their energy becomes bound. However, unbound and ever-developing energy from somatic sources is expressed in the form of drives. These drives, developing from various somatic organs, are characterized by a freedom from patterning and can be viewed in their effect upon the ego's consistent pattern of action.

If we wish to translate these statements into simpler terms applicable to my hypothesis, we must first remember that the reservoir of all instinctual forces which have psychological representation in many forms is somatic. They are visceral in origin and are communicated by nervous and humoral transmission. What happens to the whole body in its most undifferentiated state will affect those instinctual forces that through various modifications become individuated into personality and bound, those that remain free and continue to exert an active part, although variable, on the personality, and those that become differentiated into libidinal forces. All of these, whether differentiated at the time or not, should be affected in various ways by the early developmental influences imposed on the total body; and from this universal influence subsequent patterned correlations that we call psychosomatic may always be observed even after much differentiation (cf. Chapter IX).

The second category of effects on the psychological includes the influences of various types of somatic differentiation on the psychological functions after they have begun to assume ego patterns. Then delay, reality testing, synthesis of conflicting inner forces, etc., as ego functions, become easier or difficult depending upon the somatic pressures, some of which are constitutional, others stirred by external influences. Like the visiting conductor, the ego has to deal not only with the imprint of the past on itself, but has to take the somatic orchestra as it is. Some members are weak, silent or absent; others are too strong or not adjusted in timing with the whole.

When some visceral patterns are negatively conditioned and the full development of stress reactors has been restricted, a greater load is placed on what is permitted to function. Their hypertrophy may burden the ego with the task of devoting a larger share of its energy in checking such visceral responses to insure their integration and to compensate for what has become deficient. The resultant effects differ little from the defensive armoring, reaction formations, counter-cathexis with which we are so familiar. It is these defensives that give us the most reliable clues as to what visceral activity has been rigorously inhibited by early conditioning and what activity requires constant vigilance. The permitted fragments of visceral activity have become more activated as substitute outlets for energy and require greater quantities of counter-cathexis from the ego and hence more constriction of its available energy for integration and other adaptive functions. The restricted ego span becomes associated with a lack of plasticity, a greater rigidity, as well as a greater susceptibility to distintegration. As Therese Benedek (1949) states: "The ego remains at a primitive level of conditioning and when beset by too much activity for too long, eventually breaks down."

In order to summarize the hypotheses discussed above, I shall list them now in order of chronological primacy.

1. The infant is born with a significantly variable hereditary or intrinsic visceral behavior pattern that can be measured as a base line, on which subsequent influences impinge, producing alterations.

2. The neonatal organism, with whatever differentiations apparent at birth, functions viscerally as a whole with global patterns of reaction to all stress, internal or external.

3. Subsequent maturation is associated with differentiation into part-whole relations, with latency, but not extinction, of dominance of the neonatal whole pattern of functioning.

4. Such differentiation of part functions develops a new and highly individual integration of intrapersonal systems of interaction.

5. The neonatal whole pattern as well as the subsequently differentiated functions, served by neuronal nets of the vegetative nervous system, are capable of development and modification by conditioning before the advent of psychological object awareness.

6. This learning develops from stimuli emanating from the external or incorporated environment (mother, food, bacteria, medication, temperature variations, fluids or solids, quantities, etc.) and acting not only on the orifices but also on the entire visceral "in-between."

7. The first actions and subsequent reactions of the infant establish a transactional feed-back relationship of mother and child first within them as a symbiotic unit, later between them as foci. The mother is influenced by her own developmental personality derivatives, her ethnic tradition, and the current cultural values and has her own problems in maintaining an integrative capacity in relation to her child.

8. The environmental stimuli acting on the undifferentiated whole organism affect the subsequent differentiated parts, of which one is the visceral nervous system and its organ innervations, another the psychological system, even though each develops according to its natural maturational processes and receives further individual modification by special environmental influences.

9. The special influences acting on the organism, undifferentiated or in the process of differentiation by a variety of negative and positive conditioning, establish asymmetrical loading of developing smaller systems and thereby create a variety of types of integration, varying in degrees of capacity for strain under stress.

10. The later development of the psychological system, accompanying neocortical functioning, object relationship, learning by cathexis and the formation of word symbols, integrates as well as screens or reacts against the imprint of the earliest experiences, memory traces, and primary affects.

11. Regression under stress produces revival of whole organ and psychological functions with the recrudescence of primary affects expressed in primitive visceral fashion.

Hence investigation and treatment of the primary psycho-somatic (healthy or disturbed) functions in adults must revive the preverbal visceral undifferentiated total functions in which are contained the rudiments of the organ and psychological systems.

12. The stresses which re-evoke suppressed fragments of the visceral patterns and release them from integration may originate as external or internal, somatic or psychological, and traumatic, aging or the spiraling process.

The assumptions and hypotheses which I have listed do not exclude investigations by any technique or any age group, nor of any dysfunction. However, they imply the need for a multidisciplinary attack using many techniques of measurement applied to neonatal organisms and their human and physical environments through the first years of development. The focus of research on the internal aspects of differentiation, visceral learning, conditioning processes, system interactions and individuation, requires special methods of measurement of infantile visceral activities at rest and under stress. Many of these physiological and biochemical methods are now available and need only application, under controlled simultaneous observation of developing systems by a variety of co-operating investigators. Data from such an approach will give us clues as to primary psychosomatic unity and subsequent somatic and psychological variations of functions known as health or disease.

CHAPTER EIGHT

The Structure and Functions of the Mouth

MOST investigators in the psychosomatic field have been impressed by the stereotypical nature of the basic emotional constellations which are expressed in symptoms. In many formulations of psychosomatic disturbances, characterized by fluctuations related to states of emotional tension, there appear monotonously the triad of oral dependency, frustration, and oral hostility (Binger, 1951), and psychosomatic syndromes are repeatedly attributed to basic expressions of infantility and immaturity. These generalities are valid to the extent that the primary psychosomatic integrations predisposing to health and disease are present at the early undifferentiated period when the infant receives its satisfactions, tests the world of reality, and reacts to others largely with its mouth. Furthermore, the mouth as a functioning organ at first enables the infant to obtain an awareness of the nature of the world, of what is inside or outside, and how things and sensations are related. Therefore, it seems important to assemble what is known about the structure and functions of the human mouth from contributions made by many disciplines—from comparative anatomy to psychoanalysis. The compiled data have been both confusing and edifying and indicate an amazing paucity of observational and experimental methods and a large amount of unintegrated data.

The comparative anatomy of the mouth in particular, and the face in general, has been studied extensively (Rable, 1902). The primitive orifice which was destined to become the rudimentary stoma had at least three locations in metazoa before evolutionary development placed it at a pole opposite to the excretory opening. The rudimentary face and mouth serve at least five functions for primitive organisms. These include detection of desirable sources of energy, capture and preliminary preparation of energy-giving food, determination of the direction for movement toward these goals, a lure for the capture of a mate, and a gateway to the primitive gut (Gregory, 1929).

A primitive head with a complex group of sense organs by which the animal is directed to food and enabled to engulf it first developed in flatworms. True mouths first appeared in fish, arranged so that water and its solid suspensions flow in and then are eliminated through gill clefts. In some fish, lashing cilia direct the current of water inward; others, such as the lamprey, developed bony teeth for biting at objects of food. More complicated fish developed jaws and jaw muscles and a face which is essentially a bony mask. In reptilians this was overlaid by a layer of muscles. Mammals evolved a new type of mobile jaw from the homologue of the first gill arch of the fish with the appearance of the temporomandibular joint. The phylogenetic derivation of the mouth from a gill cleft is still observable in the embryological down-pocketing of outer ectoderm to meet the entoderm of the upper end of the primitive gut.

It is interesting to note that only late in evolution was the bony mask of the face overlaid with muscles. As the braincase was enlarged and the jaws receded to make for a flat face, increasingly flat as the frontal bossae extended outward and the frontal cerebral lobes increased in size, the facial muscles became overlaid by more fat and subcutaneous tissue (Keith, 1921). Mobility of the lower jaw and flexibility of facial musculature developed together as infantile dependency became prolonged and the eruption of teeth delayed. Sucking required mobility of facial musculature, which necessitated the sacrifice of armor and rigidity as protective devices for the oral opening, the source of life-preserving food. In fact, Keith and Campion (1922) state that except for the nose, the entire mammalian face is essentially part of the apparatus of mastication. Disturbances of bone formation and growth, excessive formation of lymphoid tissue in tonsils and adenoids, they believe, are concomitant and secondary to endocrine deficiency often due to infantile malnutrition. Thus, deficient primary intake of food may seriously affect later functions of the intaking apparatus.

It is not without significance that two glands of internal

secretion are derived phylogenetically and embryologically from the buccal mucosa of the oral plate. An evagination (Rathke's pouch) extends upward and backward to join an outpouching from the base of the diencephalon. The resulting structure forms the pituitary body of which the anterior lobe is derived from the buccal pouch. This lobe secretes the growth hormone, among others, and its neoplastic hypertrophy or hyperfunction results in gigantism or acromegaly, depending upon the age of onset; on the other hand, atrophic degeneration causes Simmonds' disease or generalized emaciation (Farquharson, 1950).

The thyroid gland is another branchiogenic structure which stimulates growth. It influences the basal oxygen consumption of all cells and utilizes iodine primarily obtained from ingested water. Both glands, now structuralized internally from their primitive origin in the upper alimentary tract, are concerned with growth and with maintenance of tissue activity.

Physiognomy, which was originally a science for the discovery of the disposition of the mind by the lineaments of the body, was forbidden by English law in 1743 because its practitioners were mostly rogues or vagabonds, although later, facial expressions were presumed to differentiate criminals. From Aristotle to Lombroso, character and its deviants were supposedly mirrored in fixed physical states, and in modern times, in bodily types. However, physiognomy has become specialized since the time of Bell and Darwin to the study of the face and its expressions.

Charles Darwin in his classical book (1897) enunciated three principles concerned with emotional expression:

1. The principle of serviceable associated habits—to escape danger, to relieve distress, or to achieve some desire.

2. The principle of antithesis, which postulated that movements opposite to those concerned with rage or tenseness express affection and tenderness.

3. The principle of habit, by which repeated movements become involuntary, unconscious, and utilized as means of communication, the first occurring between mother and child.

Finally, Darwin stated that the first infantile sounds varying with states of mind may determine the shape of the mouth. The idea that chronic muscular inhibition affects fullness and elasticity of the skin and may alter the contour of bones and cartilage of the face was an astonishing though rudimentary psychosomatic concept of 1872.

The principle of antithesis and subsequent symbolic representation and communication is a precursor of the gestalt theory as applied to movements (Katz, 1950) based on the neurophysiological pattern of reciprocal innervation. The snarl of anger or fear becomes the smile of pleasure on rebound. Any mother can tell you that after the red-faced infant squirms and then turns up its little mouth in a smile, it has just had a gas pain.

Muscles of expression are phylogenetically derived from the hyoid arch. They ascend and expand over the face with evolution of the pulmonary respiratory system. All these muscles are innervated by the seventh cranial nerve. Their first activity is related to the first mass-action of stepped-up respiratory functions associated with crying. At rest the newborn has little facial expression; and with infrequent blinking and tearlessness, because of late maturity of lacrimal glands, it is the counterpart of a depressed adult. The melancholic has a masked, relatively immobile face and has difficulty in crying and a general drying of lacrimal and salivary secretion. At the same time his psychodynamic tendencies are expressed in oral sucking and biting fantasies—thus psychosomatically a return to early infancy.

With all these data regarding facial expressiveness there is a curious observation which has not been explained. Domesticated animals, human infants, and most adults focus their vision on the eyes of other humans and not on the lower part of the face or other most active muscles. Those who do not look us squarely in the eye are considered shifty or guilty. Yet this is not a learned behavior since it is observable in the newborn as soon as the infant learns to fixate his eyes. Perhaps the significant quality of the eye for the stranger is the size of the pupil and the degree of tearing, both indicative of such strong and vital feelings as anxiety, rage, and sadness.

The development of teeth has been of considerable interest to orthodontists and general dentists as a basis for understanding defects of the dental arch, diseases of the teeth, and the problem of artificial dentures. Williams (1917) states that the variation of the dental arch within racial types is very small. The six anterior teeth determine the shape and size of the mouth inasmuch as they normally form an arc of a circle, but countless distortions of a perfect arc are encountered. The orbicularis oris is always slightly contracted and follows the contour of the teeth, which thus determines the mouth size and shape. Little attention has been given to the possibility that changes in innervation of the orbicularis oris effected by chronic emotional tension could influence the position and relationship of teeth and jaw. On the other hand, the position, retention, and stability of dentures is significantly affected by facial muscles (Pendleton, 1946). The orbicularis oris muscle is not well developed in the midline during the early weeks of life, which influences the choice of incision for repair of cleft lip (Logan, 1935). Actually, there is great variability of the anterior portion of this muscle beneath the epidermis, resulting in deviations in its sphincteric functions.

A condition termed rampant decay in adolescence, involving many teeth in rapid succession without known cause, has interested many dentists in psychosomatic concepts. There seems to be a high correlation between psychological factors and dental health (Manhold, 1949). Chemical changes in salivary secretion and changes in vascular caliber within the periodontal tissues may encourage bacterial activity. Neurotic need for tooth extraction to expiate a sense of guilt, fingernail or pencil biting, excessive chewing, grinding, and clenching of teeth, perverse taste for acid foods, etc., may contribute to disturbances within the oral cavity. Burning tongue and displacement of psychological conflicts to the realm of taste and smell are often of dental concern (Chavoor, 1949).

As far as I have searched, observations of early sucking patterns and type and timing of eruptions of teeth have not been reported with a view toward correlation with each other or with personalities in infancy or in later life. Yet early oral satisfactions or frustrations may give rise to soft or bitter expressions around the mouth.

Many years ago Edinger (1908) postulated a central center for "Oral Sinne" located in the tuberculum olfactorium. This was presumed to be an association area which received olfactory, tactile, gustatory, and kinesthetic impulses from the oral area and which transmitted, co-ordinated, and timed impulses to activate the motor nuclei in the medulla. In an anencephalic infant, electrically stimulated, this bulbar center was apparently sufficient for rhythmic sucking movements, because the child nursed well and lived for four days (Grinker, 1931).

It has always been a question whether oral sensibility is a conglomerate of several primary sensory modalities creating a new sensory gestalt or whether it constitutes something different and special, related to the oral cavity. It is apparent that the processes of testing the environment and, in the broadest sense, an early mastery by discriminatory acceptance or rejection of mouthed objects requires the total information obtained by several perceptive systems. But the mouth is also capable of giving warning to a vast number of digestive and metabolic functional units regarding what will be required in preparation for what is accepted.

Schuntermann (1933) showed that the mouth is capable of absorption in varying rates depending on the molecular size of various substances. Such foodstuffs stimulate the secretion of digestive juices, not only as a conditioned response with what might be called appetite secretion, but also as a response to the initial oral absorption. Depending on the rate of absorption and the type of substance mouthed, preparatory alimentary and other enzymatic secretions are stimulated. The mechanisms, functions, and modifications of such important consequences of mouth stimulation have received practically no attention.

Babkin and Van Buren (1951) consider that the motor actions of the most rostral part of the digestive tract during the ingestion of food comprise the "feeding pattern." These actions involve tongue and jaw movements, salivation and pharyngeal, laryngeal, esophageal, and gastric reflexes. A complex of reflex activities initiated by swallowing is set off from a center of deglutition in the medulla oblongata, although corticofugal impulses increase the efficiency of the complex by adapting the organism to the particular stimulus. The significant cortical center lies in the basal olfactory area which functions with the hypothalamus, subthalamus, and reticular substance of the brain stem. However, chewing and biting movements may be obtained from stimulation of the lower end of the motor cortex, especially Brodmann's area 6B. The thalamocortical pattern of oral activity is a new function superimposed on the visceral organization, capable of augmentation or inhibition.

Klüver and Bucy (1938, 1939, 1940) found striking changes in the behavior of experimental monkeys after extirpation of both temporal lobes. After the operation their animals developed psychic blindness: they could see as well as before but could not grasp or interpret the significance of the object-stimuli. Instead, they tested the world by placing all objects in their mouths, developing what Klüver calls "oral tendencies." Everything was first placed in contact with the mouth; it was then rejected if inedible, swallowed if edible. There was no discrimination through other sensations before such testing and no learning, since the same object was tested over and over again. These monkeys ate meat and other materials quite unusual for their species. Similarly, the animals seemed to be unafraid of their natural enemies or of sounds and sights which were ordinarily intensely feared. They showed marked attentiveness to all stimuli, reacting with hypermetamorphosis or compulsive behavior. Sexual activity was changed in that the monkeys were in an almost constant state of excitation, performing what for them were perversions such as fellatio and sucking ears. Their entire bodies seemed eroticized. Their total behavior was tame and they seemed devoid of fear or reaction to pain. In general after bilateral temporal lobectomy monkeys develop an "oral syndrome" because of the removal of the "visceral brain."

Klüver (1951) has recently shown that normal animals have a mechanism through which they maintain the illusion that external objects in the world are in a relatively steady state. They stay put by virtue of interrelations of brightness, size, shape, color, all subjective discriminations. When the geniculate-striate or visual system is absent, the animals are forced to fall back on functions mediated by subcortical centers. Because they are then at the mercy of ever-changing fluctuations of energy from the external environment, the old and primary testing apparatus of the mouth is reactivated.

In healthy adults, mescaline ingestion also produces oral sensations without external objects to the point of oral imagery or hallucinations. In children with unintegrated or poorly integrated perceptive systems, oral testing of external objects is maintained. In Pick's disease, in which the temporal lobes are degenerated, patients place objects in their mouths and chew incessantly. During coma induced by insulin, patients regress to behavior associated with indiscriminate licking, sucking, biting, and chewing. Post-epileptic automatisms may be accompanied by similar behavior (Grinker, 1934).

Arieti (1943) described terminal behavior in institutionalized schizophrenics similar to that shown by temporal lobotomized monkeys. In a late state of the schizophrenic process patients often lose their hallucinations and delusions and become increasingly active to the point of violence and assaultiveness. They then begin to develop bulimia with resulting great gain in weight, grabbing of food, fast eating, and ubiquitous licking activity. At first they snatch foods of choice, but later put anything into their mouths, including stones, cockroaches, inkwells, teaspoons, etc. They eject the non-edibles at first but later swallow even them. All external stimuli are reacted to by mouthing as the usual visual and auditory perceptions are ignored. They retain normal sensation in all modalities but react to pain without affect so that anesthesia is not required for surgery. These schizophrenics behave like Klüver's monkeys, and Arieti believes that the sensory input is physiologically short-circuited or that the higher nervous centers are out of function by virtue of primary or secondary degeneration.

It might be well to summarize what we have learned about the mouth from these biological data. Evolutionary processes changed the mouth from a passive intaking organ to one which is active, biting, and mobile. The bony face became mobile and physically indefensible but developed muscular activity capable of symbolically expressing fear, rage, or affection. Organs associated with the mouth in supplying substances vital for growth and the maintenance of activity became internalized in the form of glands of internal secretion. The motor or feeding patterns, in which the mouth is greatly concerned, are correlated through brain-stem centers, but their activities are augmented or inhibited by action of the cerebral cortex. Oral functions become intimately associated with all visceral motions, which are re-represented in integration with emotions through the functions of the rhinencephalon or the central visceral brain.

The primitive oral sense seems to be a perceptory gestalt in the service of testing external objects and obtaining internal sensual satisfactions. When the visceral brain is extirpated in monkeys, who have kept the world in a relatively steady state through selective visual and auditory perceptions, all sensual satisfactions become oral, objects are ingested without discrimination, and most fear of the environment is lost. This overt orality we see in humans with destruction of the temporal lobe, in persons with terminal schizophrenic states, and in very young infants. Obviously, then, "orality" has come to serve us as a symbol of certain psychological processes, which we should now examine.

CHAPTER NINE

The Psychological Implications of Oral Functions

THE MOUTH has had a significant role in myths and legends which represent man's early inner conflicts and his primitive efforts to understand and master the world about him (Frazer, 1935). The main pathway of egress for the soul was believed to be the mouth, and members of non-literate societies stopped up the mouth and nose of the deceased to hinder its departure. While yawning, the thumbs were snapped to prevent the soul from escaping. During eating or drinking there was danger that the soul would depart or some strange soul would enter; hence the mouth was kept closed as much as possible, and the house doors were kept locked. During the process of childbirth the mouths of animals were tied and people kept their mouths closed to prevent swallowing the child's soul. The early theories of sexuality, like those held by children of modern cultures, were oral. Animals or fruit, when eaten, caused impregnation in females. Children were not permitted to eat certain fruits or touch fruit trees because they would then be eating someone like themselves. Many of these myths are still to be found in rudimentary form within the rituals of some modern religions, their significance long since forgotten.

Eating and fasting became significant, according to Freud's concept of early family or clan formation, as a means of mastering forbidden tendencies and preserving taboos. The authoritative father figure was represented by a totem animal which could not be killed or eaten except at stated occasions with much ritual, in communion with all other members of the group. Repressed oral hostility was permitted expression in ceremonies combining joy with guilt. Only thus could the father image be orally attacked.

The development of mouth functions in the human infant has been studied most intensively with a descriptive method by Gesell (1937, 1942) and his co-workers. He has made reference to the legends of old by calling the mouth the "gate to the city of man-soul." Gesell's stages of development are four in number: motor behavior, adaptive behavior to new experiences, language behavior, and personal-social behavior. Within this framework he considers development as endogenous—supported, inflected, and specified by environmental factors. Mouth control is achieved by a slow and steady process of maturation which is not easily observed. The mouth is very versatile, capable of many postures and actions, beginning at the fourteenth fetal week. At birth, sucking is possible with a high degree of co-ordination. At eight weeks the infant opens his mouth for the nipple, at twelve weeks he purses his lips, at fourteen weeks he extrudes his lips to surround the nipple. By twenty weeks the lateral lower lip becomes active and can be drawn in as a spoon is removed. Following this period the various co-ordinations of chewing mature.

Over two decades ago Levy (1928), from an extensive study of infants, concluded that the most frequent cause of infantile finger and thumb sucking was insufficient lip movements because of incompleteness of the sucking phase in the feeding act. He later confirmed this in a study of puppies. The incompleteness of sucking could be attributed to spontaneous withdrawal from a too rapidly flowing nipple, forced withdrawal and hence a limited sucking time, or long intervals between the diminished time of feeding. In the few babies of that day who were on self-demand schedules, finger sucking did not develop. The severity of finger sucking was in proportion to the insufficiency of sucking time. Finger sucking developed in the first five months of life and was often followed by nail biting. Adequate lip action in sucking is the best prophylaxis against finger sucking.

Margaret Fries (1937), in addition to making direct observations on child-mother relations during feeding, has devised an oral test. This consists of presenting, removing, and restoring the nipple to the infant. Responses to this procedure are correlated with the constitutionally determined state of activity of the child, i.e., active, moderately active, or quiet. The active child startles at withdrawal and must be quieted before it accepts restoration. The moderately active child shows little disturbance at withdrawal and readily accepts the return of the nipple. The quiet infant reacts severely and must be urged to reaccept the nipple. Fries considers that these reactions have predictive value for subsequent personality development. The quiet child, for example, may develop a schizoid personality.

Hoffer (1950), points out that in about the twelfth week of postnatal life the infant discovers its hand or fingers, which may be put into its mouth, and that thus it derives auto-erotic pleasure from two sensations. This supposedly gives him a sense of self and a beginning of ego differentiation. At sixteen weeks of age, finger-to-finger sensations develop and the hand is used to relieve oral tension. By the age of three months the infant can focus on its hand and can follow movements to its mouth, has developed motor control over it, remembers its positions, and tests reality with it. Hand-to-mouth sensations may be the first nucleus of the body ego, according to Hoffer (1949).

Oral functions as significant factors in the development of personality and some of its disorders were first studied by Abraham (1927). Melancholia was his primary clinical interest, and its etiology he attributed to constitutional factors, fixations on oral satisfactions, maternal injury to infantile narcissism, and later-life repetition of disappointment. The psychological implications of oral functions now deserve our attention.

Abraham states that in sucking, infants derive satisfaction over and above fulfillment of nutritional needs. With the development of teeth, biting is also associated with erotic pleasure. These pleasures often persist in adult life in the form of direct satisfactions (eating, drinking, chewing, smoking) and as preliminary to genital satisfaction. The biting quality persists in fantasies or in cruelty, especially verbal. These qualities are exaggerated when there is an overindulgence or disappointment in infantile sucking. The overindulged may become very optimistic or over-talkative, or have an exaggerated need to be cared for. The disappointed may be envious, covetous, impatient, ambitious, and parsimonious. Early oral disappointments before primary narcissism has been satisfied and libidinization of the oedipal object attained, result in oral sadistic quality of object relationship. The object is devoured and incorporated to preserve it. This sadism colors the rudimentary superego, and the ego derived by identification becomes the object of its attacks.

Freud (1949) accepted Abraham's oral sucking and biting phases as factors in personality development. His over-all statement is that the early body or visceral ego is based on memory traces, for although the id is hereditary and the superego is cultural, the ego is derived from the subject's own experiences. These experiences may be erotic and aggressive, sometimes both combined in the same biological function, such as eating plus sensuality. The infantile organism receives internal perceptions, from diverse and deep strata of the body, which are more fundamental and elementary than external perceptions and influence psychological states even when consciousness is not clear. Body perceptions arise from different places simultaneously and may have different or opposite qualities. They remain silent when gratified, for nothing is impelling about pleasure. The ego is first and foremost a body ego—not merely a surface entity, but the projection of many internal surfaces.

Melanie Klein (1932) developed unusually startling abstract concepts of infantile psychology. These were based not on observational studies but on reconstructions from childhood analysis. The details of her theories are buried in incomprehensible mixtures of inaccurate technical jargon, but they have been unraveled by Glover (1945) in a comprehensive criticism. Yet Klein has performed a service in calling attention to the early development of the oedipus complex and the early appearance of the superego or its forerunner. Cogent to our subject are the mechanisms by which the infant presumably deals with its human world. Initial oral frustration releases sadism with fantasies of swallowing or introjecting good and bad parts of the mother's body and its contents, followed by attempts to eject them. The main point is that swallowing and regurgitation are the prototypes of psychological functions, literally conceived.

Glover (1924), in discussing the significance of the mouth in psychoanalysis, considers three functions of the oral stage: libidinal development, body-ego development, and isolation or fusion of impulses of destruction. He makes quite clear the idea that orality is not an isolated stage but has temporarily a relative primacy. A direct quotation of his brilliant expressions may be illuminating. "The oral stage commences with certain prescribed functions to perform, to sweeten the pill of existence and to afford repetition situations, such as the ever repeated gratifications and privations of sucking and hunger, whereby the catastrophic primal experience of birth is worked through. Both of these serve a third purpose, viz. to link the subject more and more to the outer world. The first is libidinal, the second repetitive, and the third the reality function of oral development."

Lewin (1950) describes the oral triad as the wish to devour, the wish to be devoured, and the wish to sleep. These, he believes, are primarily memory traces of physiological states at the nursing or sucking stage. Biting is due to frustration of sucking, and the eruption of teeth does not demarcate a special phase of orality. In manic attacks biting is an aggressive effort to get to the breast or to repel the thwarting environment; there is the wish to devour with a denial of the other two components, which are overlaid with anxiety. Like Klüver's monkeys and Arieti's terminal schizophrenics, the baby tests reality by placing objects in its mouth. Lewin, however, decries the use of oral terminology in psychology as if the outer world were swallowed and the inner world a stomach. Reality is represented by early memory traces of oral, later sensorimotor, and still later symbolic and conceptual models, with increasing renunciation of instinctual satisfactions. "The world becomes progressively less edible." In states of ego regression or sleep, the actual or synthetic dream is composed of an oral screen with sensorimotor pictorialization and symbolic ideas. For revival of oral satisfaction, reliving is the only effective means—and this is the means the manic adopts.

This is the point at which to summarize the way the mouth appears psychologically. The mouth was first considered not only the passageway for necessary food and for the soul, but also as the path for impregnation and the means of devouring the needed, feared, loved, and hated mother and father. Today psychoanalysis postulates little more in its triad of functions: maintenance of life, sensual satisfaction, and aggressive mastery of reality. However, major advances in modern times are the concepts of mouth functions in determining the structure and stability of the personality. Anthropological, observational, and psychoanalytical methods have been directed toward determining the interrelationship between child and mother, mouth and nipple. Most modern psychoanalysts, whether studying myths, legends, dreams and associations, or nonliterate man, have tended to consider the physiological operations of the mouth as literal rudiments of psychic functions. From Abraham to Lewin the language, if not the intent, implies psychological sucking, biting, vomiting, digestion, defecation—sometimes with substitute terms such as incorporation, introjection of part or whole objects, or projection. Perhaps there are other ways by which we may correlate early mouth functions, as related to food and physical objects, with psychological processes and psychic structures.

All psychoanalysts and psychiatrists have been forced, if not willing, to heed the clinical data concerned with physical and psychological aspects of mouth functions as they are expressed with varying degrees of directness. There is no need to recapitulate clinical experiences or to outline the typical current psychodynamic formulations that we apply to the processes termed regression to oral stages. This phenomenon exists in many forms from excessive eating (bulimia) to not eating (anorexia), in dreams, fantasies and overt behavior concerned with storage, retention, or elimination of food, of mother as a whole object, or of mother's breast. Furthermore, in these regressive states up to the point of almost complete collapse of ego functions, there is an increasing sense of guilt and depression. The closer to direct expression of eating, the more severe the superego pressure becomes.

I should now like to consider the development of body and psychological ego as a transactional process involving infant and mother to determine how much the mouth really participates.

There is no sharp dividing line between the natural maturing processes associated with physical and psychological growth and those facilitated by experiences or learning, which we term development. Neither is there a crucial separation in time between the stimulus-response behavior resulting in conditioning and the special human kind of learning through meaningful relations with objects. These seem to be co-operating processes persisting in different proportions throughout life. But before learning can occur from object interaction or from even more specialized and evolved autonomous ego function, there must naturally be an ego capable of relationships and autonomy. The essential features of primary development and learning are related to the influence of experience arising from various sources and quantities of external supply of energy acting on specific receptor and action systems. In this presentation only the external maternal energy source and the sensorimotor system of the mouth are considered.

Let us take as our simplest model the transactions of a single cell and its environment. Inner needs for sources of supply of energy motivate random movements in search of necessary substances. When found, needed sources of supply outside the living semipermeable membrane are permitted to pass through, and larger objects are engulfed by the flow of pseudopodia around them. Some of these substances are immediately utilized, others are stored for future use, so that a continuous process of transition of substances results. Adverse changes in the external milieu stimulate a greater need for excess food for preservation as storage. Through such incorporation the organism becomes better able to withstand deprivation and stress, and its dependence on an ever adequate external source of needed supply is decreased. Intracellular storage is, therefore, a rudimentary emancipation from the vagaries of the environment.

Inside the cell, metabolic chemical processes convert the ingested mass into utilizable forms of energy. By-products of reduced substances are constantly in the process of discharge; when discharge is not possible, the foreign body must be retained within the cell. Although dangerous objects are generally avoided or prevented from inward passage, when perchance they are incorporated, they are encapsulated and kept separate from the main body of cytoplasm.

What now can be considered the organism itself and what constitutes its environment? Outside the cell are objects which in the future may be incorporated and others which in the past have been within or part of the cell and have been eliminated. Inside the cell, substances which have been taken in are in various stages of utilization; in fact, in process of becoming cell in future time or of having been cell in past time. Thus both outside and within, boundaries of life are indistinct and mass-energy relationship is a gradient within the space-time continuum. Organismic-environmental dichotomy becomes an artificiality. From this model we may now jump in evolutionary time to the living mouth-child and its environmental supply of nipple-mother.

The infant's first need, over and above the air which it automatically inspires, is for food. It already has a built-in neurological feeding pattern of unconditioned reflexes, correlated in lower centers, capable of functioning at birth. Satisfaction of this need relieves tension and is followed by a quiescent period of sleep. Lack of satisfaction or incomplete satisfaction results in persistence or even increase of tension accompanied by random behavior of the total organism as though it were reacting to stress. These are the first infantile responses which validate the basic pleasure-pain principle of the undifferentiated organism. At this stage the infant has little if any differentiation or awareness of self as a total entity. Since only mouth and contact sensibilities are matured and distant objects cannot be perceived, the chief expression of its drives is toward the goal of incorporation of food within the mouth. Where does the environment begin and the individual end?

Inner needs energize drives which push the organism to search for stimuli or to accept those impinging on it, for the decrement of tension and the experience of pleasure. An external object of supply is a necessity for the derivation of satisfaction, and its presence is intimately linked to the complex of *need-searching* for *tension-reduction*. Indeed, primary learning theory postulates the complex as *need-response-reduction* of tension. The sensation acquired from the responding object and its supply, as well as its image or memory, is probably associated with that part of the body through which the aim of the physiological drive is expressed or satisfied. Need building up to *tension-experience* through gastric hunger contraction, salivation, lip sensations, etc., and object *reducing-tension* through sensations of nipple between lips, mouth filled with milk, deglutition represent a single psychosomatic complex.

Psychologically the resulting satiation pleasure or satisfaction constitute an erotic system in which the response from the object (mother) becomes experienced as love and the body sense (lips) as sensual or erotic. It would be difficult to determine how much of the erotic system is organism and how much is object, but the satisfaction leads to a preservation of the image within the rudimentary organism and becomes part of the developing self. If there is failure or delay in completing reduction of tension, the primitive fear-rage (pain) excitation develops. This somatic reaction is the prototype of anger, and hostility is represented by the unsatisfying object. If tension increases, fear becomes the representative of the object and anxiety that of the subject. Lewin (1950) has stated this in another way in his formulation which considers that eating and being eaten are undifferentiated. Whether representative of body or object, the reactions to frustration and increase in tension are painful. At a not too much later stage there develops a tendency to isolate these painful phenomena from the self and attach them to an external object, at first unstably and later firmly by the mechanism of projection.

In this phase of maturation, reality, as far as the organism is concerned, exists only within itself, partly pleasurable, partly painful, depending upon the satisfactory or unsatisfactory experiences which the primary drives meet. One may compare this concept semantically with Klein's (1932) introjection of good and bad part-objects. In any language this is the stage of primary preverbal learning. It is only briefly limited to responses experienced by the mouth, because tactile, pain, auditory, visual, and vibratory perceptual systems very quickly participate in the child-mother relationship. The energy from which the drives develop, cathect that part of the body which expresses needs and receives degrees of satisfaction and becomes a component of the body-ego nucleus which ever remains ingrained and constant, and able to reappear under regressive conditions. Its constancy corresponds with the formulations of Freud, Herold (1941–1942), and Benedek (1953), who state that the nucleus of the ego is a body ego (one might say subject and maternal body), whose activities, with those of the instincts, are in the service of metabolism. However, at this early age they undergo their greatest vicissitudes, becoming distorted in aim, direction, and object. Such permanent alterations are precursors in the formation of specific personalities on which the continuous free energy of other drives and the cathexis of interpersonal relations operate later. A suitable analogy is the process of mountain development by a new volcano. The first eruptions of lava after cooling leave behind a structural remnant which is repeatedly modified by subsequent eruptions. The final pattern may be predicted from the interaction of the earliest outflows on a particular terrain.

The primitive form of learning that has been discussed is the prototype for conditioned responses which depend upon the degree of evocation of fear responses, the development of symbolic cues, and the reinforcement and extinguishing of responses by gratification or unsatisfaction of the aims of drives. Without discussing conditioning further, we can say that behaviorists have recently concluded that conditioned experimental animals develop memory images of stimulus-response patterns and search for them, attempting to find cues to set off the entire behavior complex (Tolman, 1951). There is a great need to understand more of the internal psychodynamics of primitive conditioning processes.

Mouth functions exist in the service of obtaining needs, testing objects for utility or danger and for what they are, and the sensual pleasure of excess stimulation, in isolation for a short time since other sensory modalities soon become activated. What is called the oral stage exists during the period of intrinsic primary activity and is much more than oral, but includes in addition to a complicated motor apparatus for mastery over objects placed in the mouth, other perceptive systems which serve as avenues of input. They do not generate energy of drives but are activated by them. It is thus completely erroneous to talk about oral libido, regressed libido, or, for that matter, libido as *arising from* any discrete organ or zone. When other receptive systems mature and the child now reacts rather than exclusively acts, primitive percepts remain isolated for a time as unintegrated rudiments of the body ego. In some children with anatomical lesions of the midbrain such integration is never possible and higher learning is limited so that they often behave as if feeble-minded, although the cerebral cortex is well developed and newer methods of teaching establish the fact of learning ability. As the normal child's integrative capacity matures, discrete images of self and self-experiences fuse into a whole.

The next stage of development brings us to a new and human quality described as identification through meaningful attachments to significant other humans. Before this point is reached the important differentiation psychologically between self and not-self has already occurred. Freud discussed this process in his delineation of the development of the superego through introjection. Social scientists have been much interested in this formulation, since it was the first systematic presentation of the influence of culture and social values on the formation of personality (Parsons, 1951a). The model applies equally well to the development of the psychological ego and ego-ideal.

This form of learning depends upon the ability to use and understand cognitive and expressive symbols at a time when maternal attitudes are understood and interpreted as pleasurable or displeasurable; there then develops the beginning of love and the capacity to endure delay, frustration, and discipline. Between mother and child there exists a two-way system for the intercommunication of expressions of feeling. The child can understand proscriptions and prohibitions and recognize his own responsibility in what people feel about him (Parsons, 1951a). It is at this point, when the original symbiosis of mother-child is broken and the child figuratively "walks away on his own," that he has to accept signals from a distant mother, not one who is part of him. Then his ego-ideals develop, along with more or less "shame-anxiety" (Piers and Singer, 1953).

In the development of the ego, ego-ideal, and superego, objects are not introjected or taken into the personality. Only symbols of memory traces of *relationships* are internalized after a process of cognition, appraisal, and cathexis. Identification does not mean becoming or incorporating the object and affects, but involves actions which have become organized from experience with cultural patterns. Internalization is achieved in terms of feelings toward objects (people), and in terms of the value of the relationship. Here too incorporation and introjection as derived from physical oral ingestion are inadequate concepts.

In maturation, symbolic pictures, words, and abstractions add to, screen, or overlay the visceral components of the body ego and the primitive affects of the psychological ego; but these do not vanish, for they reappear under many conditions. When objects can be perceived at a distance and brought close to the organism, avoided, or repelled, newer forms of relationship and mastery are available. In addition more evolved autonomous ego functions may permit a type of learning freed from the strains of dealing with sexual and aggressive forces (Hartmann, 1950). However, severe trauma, premature stress, or forced maturation may break down the ego's defensive capacities for avoidance, and denial or not looking may result in regression to primitive touching and sucking forms of testing.

Perhaps the stages of relationships that I have described

may be stated in summary in another manner. The receptive and perceptive functions available to the growing child fall into cognitive hierarchies of cues, signs, and symbols. The cognitive pattern expands in organization—it assembles with ever-increasing organization. For our frame of reference such higher elaborations are dependent upon distance from the mother (a function of physiological aging) and the capacity for distant forms of two-way communications. Eventually systems of approval-disapproval develop, creating ego-ideals and shame; systems of morals and ethics develop influencing conscience and guilt. Both of these forces—shame and guilt—become internalized and constituent parts of the personality through accretions to the primary assembly of body and psychological ego, of which the body ego is primary. When such an assembly breaks down as a result of stress the arrangement of its parts assumes a different form, rather than a regression in an orderly fashion. The primitive body ego again assumes primacy and the burden of communication returns to the contact sensibilities. Even though the early patterns of relationship return, the acquired differentiation does not necessarily disappear entirely and a psychosis develop. Revival of oral patterns, especially when cannibalistic, is often associated in depressions with severe superego anxiety. Revival of early sucking attitudes may evoke shame anxiety from still active ego-ideals.

The initiation of current interest in the mouth comes from its significance to psychosomatic theory. The preceding theoretical discussion indicates how primary experiences seem to affect the psychosomatic organization in the formation of the body ego and how the development of psychological ego and superego occurs through affective experiences. In neither process is there a direct homologue with the biology of eating or orality. What happens at first suggests that neither past nor present environment can be fractured from the organism and that none of the past can be considered as gone or lost. What can be lost are complex assemblies of transaction suitable for current object relationships, which release past relationships and past child-mother patterns. Disappointments, if severe enough, may overcome integrative successes and force regression to earlier patterns of relationships and often to psychosomatic patterns characteristic of specific mother-child experiences. When the breast or bottle is lost in weaning, when loved objects are lost or separation from them is threatened, in short when one misses or loses an important object or cannot solve a real problem, what is always present although hidden may become reactivated. As in the case of the phantomization of an amputated limb, those who are thus severely disappointed—which means those who have never achieved an intrapsychic separation from the mother and developed egos of their own capable of real object relationship—revive the child-mother or mouth-nipple pattern.

The closer to the eating pattern, the more primitive the ego, the more sadistic the superego, and the more alimentary and depressed the person. What has been included in the last sentence is true to the clinical data but is nevertheless a vast and unknown field about which little that is definite may be stated. Closeness to the primary eating pattern means a return to a period when body and psychological egos were maturing and developing. Regression to this phase does not mean the development of a psychosis, as some would state, even though behavior may at times seem psychotic. The integrative functions of the ego still persist, although weakened and silent, and can be relatively quickly resuscitated. The sadistic nature of the superego corresponds to the image of the disappointing and weaning mother in the light of the physical and psychological meaning to the infant at that time. Demanding subject and frustrating object are one complex, so that suffering of deprivation and reaction to it are all *inside* and *hurting*.

As has been mentioned before, the depressed patient and the newborn have many similiarities. They are dry-eyed and facially unexpressive, and presumably both are concerned with fantasies of sucking or biting. Psychosomatic disturbances of varying degrees of regression are all related to quantitative levels of hypersecretion (wetness) plus hypermotility and hyperemia. The development of free fluid which is the homologue of weeping may be shifted by spontaneous psychological means or hypnosis from organ to organ. Contrasted with depression, psychosomatic disturbances are wet instead of arid and, as we see so often, depressed patients begin to recover as they become able to weep. It seems that the reciprocal relationship between depression (and mania) on the one hand, and psychosomatic disorders on the other, needs more clarification than the current formulations supply. It would seem to be that the crying but non-weeping infant and the depressive are completely given up to self, not cognizant of any not-self, waiting passively and hopelessly for sources of supply, unable to differentiate angry self from hostile depriver. On the other hand, the psychosomatic patient weeps or secretes fluid, asking for supply from others or giving to himself in fantasy, with appropriate pouring out of fluid as a primitive means of maintaining homeostasis. According to this formulation, his reaction corresponds to a stage when awareness of separation between self and not-self has already developed.

We may now speculate as to why psychosomatic disturbances are on the increase in our Western culture, assuming that the increase is not due to better case-finding and modern diagnosis. To a great extent our identification with the father and the corollary participation of the father in the formation of the superego has decreased. This in itself is the result of socio-economic influences which have changed family structure and function. The father is simply not the dominant or co-dominant factor in child development or discipline. He cannot be depended on as a source of strength, a protector from the too strong positive or negative attitudes toward the mother, and he fails to exert pressure for growth and responsibility. In our culture, negative feelings toward the father are less a residue of the oedipus conflict. They are more a combination of anger at the father's failure to save the child from the possessive and infantilizing and often feminizing role of the mother toward the boy, and in his case, resentment for the frustration in his subsequent passive position. In both sexes, the superego, if derived more from the mother, functions as a superimposition of the rudimentary pre-oedipal superego, accentuating its effects without the neutralization of a masculine relationship. The erotic and aggressive components of infant-mother relationship, imprinted on the infantile psychosomatic unit, continue to manifest themselves on somatic and psychic systems as they develop each according to its pattern. The psychic system now receives another dose of almost exclusive mother relationship, overloading its capacity to handle its simultaneous erotic and aggressive components. The result is a breakdown of differentiation and a regressive return, in part, of a psychosomatic unity in which relationships are communicated, experienced, and reacted to with an overwhelming somatic participation.

Thus we may derive implications for therapy in that psychosomatic disturbances require not less but more penetration into the deeper levels of the organism's mental structure. They require penetration far beyond the nuclear oedipal conflict of classical psychoanalysis into the vast area of pregenitality or the age of succorance. To reach this, verbal screens must be penetrated and preverbal affective symbolic behavior must be understood. This problem is as difficult, although not the same, as is that of the schizo-phrenic. New techniques and new forms of symbolism for therapeutic communications will probably have to be de-vised.

Has the natural history, anatomy, physiology, and my-thology of the mouth added anything to our use of oral con-cepts in the theory of development of healthy and sick per-sonalities? The more we have learned about the structure and function of the mouth in the human organism, the more dissatisfaction there is with our current psychoana-lytic formulations. Some things are clear: In psychology we have considered mouth functions too literally, we have neg-lected to evaluate properly other systems of mastery, per-ception, and sensuality, and we have considered mouth functions as isolated. For psychological purposes it would be better if we paid less attention to the mouth as a single area of action and considered the potentialities of the entire organism as a projection of many surfaces—not a surface (Freud). All inner processes enter into transactional rela-tionships with the environment at the surfaces of the body where they can be experienced. The biological and psycho-logical organization of infant and mother and what goes on between them at all surfaces needs extensive research.

Most animals utilize the energy of the universe directly by ingesting the organic matter derived from other living or previously living organisms; man is able to utilize the energy of the world in ways other than eating. Many animals and infants test the universe with their mouths; man is able to test the external world and learn its meanings through distant receptors which he has extended to infinity by his own inventions. Primitive man's mythology or interpretation of his position in the universe was mostly oral (internalized or projected); modern man's view of the world is in addition transactional and communicative.

Psychiatry, psychosomatic medicine, psychology, and all those disciplines that should be considered together as "behavioral science" should now be able to go beyond the zonal, especially oral, concepts of mastery. Certainly human infants recapitulate in their ontogenetic development the primary use of oral processes in their earliest state of undifferentiated psychosomatic functions, and these patterns reappear in regressive states. However, when the processes of the highly differentiated psychological systems are observed and evaluated, we should now be able to use the concepts of transactional communications with signs and symbols as more suitable for our present intellectual needs. We shall now turn to the discussion of integrations, transactions, and field theory.

CHAPTER TEN

Integration and Field Theory

IN A PREVIOUS chapter it was suggested that the natural focus for investigation of psychosomatic processes was the period of differentiation from the original primordial psychosomatic unity and the subsequent integration of the differentiated parts into a new and individualized whole. Differentiation has already been discussed in Chapters VI and VII. We shall now turn our attention to the integrative processes, recognizing that their directions, quantities, and timing are already individually specified by hereditary and early environmental factors. Nevertheless, the extensive similarities among members of a species, as determined by the available intrinsic apparatus and its capacities, permit many valid generalizations about patterns.

Biological or living organisms have been characterized as open systems, in contrast to closed physical systems, by Bertalanffy (1950). In a closed system energy or mass does not enter, reversibility occurs, and entropy is at its theoretical maximum. In living, open systems there is a continuous exchange of energy with the environment; irreversibility, growth, and steadiness are characteristic, and negative entropy predominates. Organic systems rapidly transform and bind energy within units permeable to permit an exchange of substance across their living boundaries in both directions. Thus, living organisms are open and in circular process with their environments. These energy systems are in constant but variable states of activity. They utilize energy to obtain, incorporate, and alter substances from the environment. By so doing, they store energy and create new organizations of mass. The intermediate aspects of this change of organization of non-living substances is the liberation internally of utilizable energy which varies in space and time within its parts, characteristic of a mobile system of gradients (Child, 1921). Between these parts are constant circular processes of interaction and communication.

It seems that of these various activities the highest or most intense (chemically, electrically) is most internal or central to the organization and most concerned with the processes of change of internalized substances. On the other hand, the area of lowest activity coincides with the living periphery of the organization which is in process or functional relationship with the environment or the non-individual, whether or not this is another living organism. This area functions in reaching and preparing for incorporation of selected new substances to obtain more sources of energy, and to avoid or destroy interference or danger from the environment. Intrinsic tensions activate the embryonic organism before any sensorial apparatus in communication with the environment is developed or in function. The primary source of action of the living unit arises from an internal energy system which is the stimulus for the first interactions and exchanges of the organism with its environment; only later do perceptive systems evolve and function in this process. Thus, constitutionally derived, wound-up activity of the organization facilitates its existence before exteroceptive functions develop.

It is not possible for me to discuss these intracellular processes in greater detail, for these involve a specialized knowledge of the complicated fields of enzymatic biochemistry. In the multicellular organism many enzymes are liberated by cells in various tissues for extracellular, humeral diffusion. They comprise a complicated system of activators with multiple precursors, co-enzymes, and complicated chains of checking and reversing antagonistic enzymes, all of which in health seemingly balance each other to facilitate the conversion of substances for utilizable energy, to store energy, and to mobilize metabolic processes under specific circumstances. Study of these energy systems has disclosed strange and intricate complexities to which there seems no end or beginning.

In most organisms, hormonal secretions are liberated through the function of more specialized organs. They add certain new functions and activate and integrate the intracellular and extracellular enzymatic systems, particularly during periods of stress and development, growth and decline.

In even more evolved organisms, a nervous system subserves faster and more variegated types of internal integrations and transactions with the environment. The specialized properties of these highly differentiated nervous structures are their greater degree of irritability and speed of conductivity. The nervous system rapidly conducts internally those environmental stimuli which act on the body through special sensory end organs and cells. Large groups of body cells far distant from the source of stimulation are set into action from the same environmental stimulus. Other portions of the nervous system conduct impulses through effector fibers and excite large groups of muscular structures and secretory cells into activity. Interposed between the sensory and effector functions are integrating and correlating centers with multiple complex intercommunications concomitant with a corresponding organismal evolution. With this increasing complexity there develop a greater number of possible responses to a single stimulus.

The end organs on which the environmental stimuli impinge are adapted to respond to specific types such as touch, pain, temperature, etc., within a limited quantitative range. Although each organism has a basic property or irritability, it also has a selective sensitivity. Furthermore, external stimuli do not influence the intensity of nerve response. The quantity of energy firing and traversing the nerve fiber is constant to its capacity. No matter how strong the stimulus may be, if the nerve fiber responds at all, it will respond with few exceptions in the same quantity to its maximum; this is the "all-or-none" law. We can conclude not only that the organism selects the energy (stimulation) it accepts from the environment but also that it maintains its own rate of responsiveness. This constitutes a biological and effective rudimentary defense against disintegration. Turning to the central and effector aspects of conduction, various muscular or glandular activities are discharged through a final common nerve pathway which is fired by stimuli from the central nerve net. From this net, composed of multiple long and short reverberating circuits, depending on the type and degree of external stimulation, activity expresses a central quantitative summation or impedance of subliminal charges. Innumerable gradations of effects are possible depending upon the time of discharge and the number of discharging motor units (Lillie, 1945). The effect is thus the resultant of timing and quantity of summation rather than of any special quality of nerve response.

The autonomic or visceral nervous system is more directly concerned with storage and mobilization of energy to and from the large bodily reservoirs. One portion mobilizes the resources of the body for emergency mass-discharge under varying conditions of stress. The other is more conservative and synthetic in its functions and activates more discrete units. However, these divisions function together (like enzymes, co-enzymes and antagonistic enzymes), balancing or summating each other, controlling otherwise rapid changes of energy, subserving thereby a tendency toward a steady state. This autonomic nervous system is closely integrated with higher nervous centers, which have evolved later, and participates in many other bodily functions and in response to internal and external sensory stimuli.

The higher autonomic or sympathetic centers were primarily developed in association with the sense of smell, which projected the animal forward in space and time to permit it to become aware of future danger. Their anatomical position in the 'tween-brain or diencephalon places them at the crossroads between the higher cortical centers, with their sensitivity to greater ranges of satisfaction and stress, and the body's machinery for response and adjustment. At this level of irritability, danger from without (fear), or from within (anxiety), extends the function of organ sensitivity to the highest degree. Here, actions which constitute responses in adjustment to stress, are capable of being set off by symbolic representations of remembered dangers.

The 'tween-brain contains relatively discretely localized centers for the discharge and conservation of energy, acting together in a co-operative fashion. Nor is activity limited to visceral functions when these centers detonate, for with increasing needs or severer stress, discharges flow to the somatic division of the nervous system, and striped muscular movements result. If the level of excitation reaches a certain threshold, responses occur in the form of violent aggressive striking, or fighting or rhythmic running movements. Also, the need for food to build up energy reservoirs may necessitate aggressive and grabbing, intaking movements. Thus, in the service of need or of response to danger, in attempting to maintain a steady inner state, aggressive (motor) systems are activated, but this, in effect, is only a quantitative increase within an energy system which functions to maintain itself.

The property of irritability within living protoplasm is magnified and specialized by the nervous system, but no new quality is added. The nervous system hastens energy exchange and widens its effects. By virtue of private pathways from end organs it tries to order selectively what part of the environment is permitted to act on the organism (Klüver, 1951), and thereby tends to keep the environment in a steady state (from the frame of reference of the organism). Its rate of response permits control over the rate of energy exchange, and it activates its motor control in varying degrees and rhythms. From the single living cell to the cerebral cortical mantle, energy systems are in a constant state of flux, and apparent differences in direction of flow are only indications of an integrated pattern at a given time, since all directions are always concurrently present. These are not polar opposites of different systems but quantitative variations of a single complex energy exchange within the organismic-environment gestalt.

However, the human nervous system consists not only of correlating and conducting centers with their peripheral receptors and effectors. The cortical mantle has been associated with the intensification of functions which permit the living organization a great mastery of time and space, involving memory of the past and projection into the future, and the capacity for more choice instead of rigidly stimulus-bound action. Many physiological properties have been ascribed to the cerebral cortex, as one would expect, with its concomitant complicated psychological functions, but it is doubtful that these represent any basic differences from other organic systems. Therefore, we should turn our attention to the psychological patterns and see in what way and to what degree they reflect or re-represent the biological integrative processes.

We frequently assume that psychological activities utilize and bind energy like any other organic process. Sherrington's remarks tended to negate this when he wrote (1941): "The mental is not examinable as a form of energy. As followers of natural science we know nothing of any relation between thoughts and the brain except as a gross correlation in time and space." On the other hand, Adrian (1918) states: "Mental interaction systems are but higher forms of intra-cellular enzymatic systems." Coghill hypothesized: "In the organic sphere the total pattern has three constituent components, structure, function and mentation. These three components of the living organism undergo varying degrees of individuation. Structure is fundamentally spatial. Function is primarily temporal. Mentation in its highest degree of individuation conforms to neither space nor time." It is at this point of the "more-than-organic function" that the space-time continuum in the organismic-environmental gestalt becomes less clear and a new language has to be devised. Because of the lack of perceptive systems by which we may observe the mental clearly, analogical terms have been used and concepts have been manipulated by "it is as if."

The most earnest attempt to fit the psychological into a biological conceptual scheme has been made by Freud and his students. They attempt a transition from the internal biological organization of "instincts" or intrinsic energy systems to the psychological "drives," attributing to the latter a borderline integrative status between the physical and the mental. According to Freudian concepts, the drives are more flexible, mobile, and capable of delay. Their aims or objects are interchangeable and are capable of quantitative variation, of inhibition of aim, of turning to the opposite, etc. The Freudian psychological model demonstrates considerable congruence with biological concepts. The organism has specific needs which, when satisfied, release tension and afford pleasure; the sum of excitation or so-called psychic energy is quantitatively fixed; there is a tendency for the organism to maintain a state of constancy; there are gradients of energy or tension and hierarchies of organs used for its discharge; there is an orderly system of development of part-functions and in maturity an integration of these functions into a new organic whole, with stress producing disintegration and the revival of old part-functions. The classification of drives as belonging to id or ego, self or race preservation, libidinal or aggressive, is dependent upon frames of reference and indicates less a distinction of forms of energy than variations of direction perceived from changing positions of the observer. The Freudian psychology conceives of a constitutionally derived inner organization which first functions without stimuli from the external environment, the so-called id. The development of later, more complicated reactivity with the environment, as in the total organism after its perceptive systems have developed, is a function of the ego which is sensitive to both internal and external stimuli and develops its capacities from a learning, self-corrective process in transaction with the living and physical world about it. It then becomes the functioning organization which perceives inner tension and outer stress, and has the power of permitting or inhibiting action and synthesizing conflictual tendencies. "Thus beginning with internally derived instinctual forces having to do with the growth, development, and survival of the individual and of the species, we see the evolution from the single cell to the multicellular organism, with subordination of the parts to the whole, and from the relatively isolated to the highly social organism, with the subordination of the organism to the group. There is a continuity between the biologic, psychologic and social evolution" (Engel, 1953).

To summarize the above-mentioned basic processes I have stated them in succinct outline form opposite terms of abstraction most suitable to each function. (See page 152.)

What we know (and our lacunae are bridged by assumptions) indicates that from the intracellular enzymes to the psychological forces operating through the cortical mantle,

Energy binding	Organisms rapidly transform energy, binding it in utilizable form, developing therewith structuralized patterns of differentiations which are maintained in a relatively steady state,
Differentiation	
Steady state	demarcated from their environments
inner ⎱ defense against	and defended against disintegration
outer ⎰ disintegration	by living semipermeable boundaries
Circular process	through which circular corrective
Communication	processes of transaction take place
Value systems	with varying rate and rhythm inherent in their structuralized patterns,
Sensitivity	possessing the characteristics of sen-
Responsiveness	sitivity and responsiveness, and their appropriate action systems, inte-
Part-whole relationship	grated with their environments to
Integration	form larger systems, thereby sacrific-
Expansion (goal-changing)	ing some overt autonomy.

integration of part functions tends to maintain the organism in a steady internal state and in equilibrium with its environment. For humans, the processes of adjustment between the individual and the environment are most flexible because of the high degree of psychological development and the evolution of the symbolic process. It furnishes a most delicate instrument to measure variations in the pattern of environmental processes and to institute changes in the opposite direction serving to maintain a steady state or "adjustment." The psychological processes maintain the total organism in equilibrium (integration) with its environment within larger extents of time and space.

Our assumptions that the human organism is part of and in equilibrium with its environment, that its psychological processes assist in maintaining an internal equilibrium and that the psychological functioning of the organism is sensitive to both internal needs and external conditions, bring us to the realization that a large aspect of psychosomatic organization has been neglected by most observers. Our analysis of previous investigations has indicated that their focus has been on unidirectional, linear causal chains, on interrelationships or correlations between two functions, or on some genetic aspect. Although the latter is essential to the understanding of the processes of differentiation and of integration, the actual functioning of the organism cannot be understood except by a study of its transactional processes as occurring in a total field. Although the unfractured field can give few indications of its genic, maturational, or developmental history, since it deals with time as of present action, the study of successive fields from birth to maturity furnishes a longitudinal dimension to multiple cross sections.

The unitary nature of organismic environment in space and time as an action system has been particularly emphasized by Dewey (1946) and Bentley (1950) and more recently by the latter in his so-called kennetic inquiry. "This is a name proposed for organized investigation into the problem of knowings and knowns, where this is so conducted that the full range of subject matters—all the knowings and knowns—form a common field." He divides scientific inquiry into three fields, physical, physiological, and behavioral or psychological, in which the techniques of appraisal and the language of reports at present are not interchangeable. As one reads the language of Bentley the complexity, the unnaturalness of syntax and the number of multihyphenated words necessary to maintain the concept of an unfractured field are disconcerting. It is apparent that contemporary man is under the greatest of strains in conceiving himself subjectively in process, as part of and in transaction with his environment, and in losing his selfness, his "I-ness," his boundaries even in fantasy.

This difficulty has been raised by Scott in a discussion of the body scheme. Scott (1949) compared schizophrenic patients who were concerned with their souls, minds, and bodies, and searched for some sort of unity or integration with their environments or reality, and patients with oceanic feelings or a sense of cosmic consciousness located somewhere in space. Some felt that they had been engulfed by the world; others had swallowed the world. In contrast with the elated feeling associated with this cosmic fantasy is the catastrophic chaos of the depressed or paranoid patient who feels himself completely isolated and differentiated from the rest of the human world.

The human organism at birth has only primitive awareness of selfness or I-ness. With the process of development this total pattern is differentiated with the body integument as the living interface between processes within and without. As this occurs the I or the self develops and even becomes differentiated into many parts such as the multiple I's of various social roles, depending upon the external situation and its demands. At any biological or psychological level such structuring or organization is either a by-product or the cost of a more specialized function. From a whole system in process with the environment there develops a transactional relationship of parts of the self with the whole and with the environment, but not against unless in a psychosis, sometimes in sleep or infrequently in temporary phases of ecstasy or elation, does the boundary of the self diminish (never to disappearance). Hence one has to become almost psychotic to approach a frame of reference in which the organismic-environmental gestalt can be subjectively perceived. In the temporal aspects of the environmental field, the past is structuralized in memory patterns, the future is mysterious, and the present absorbs all our perceptive systems. All are pictorially represented in our mental processes by space dimensions which can only be remembered or anticipated by projecting our present bodies forward or backward. It is no wonder that of the three aspects of the space-time field, we as individuals, in groups, or in societies select one to think, dream, fantasy of and to place greater value on, and that unified concepts are so difficult to arive at and to maintain in science.

Cantril, Ames, Hastorf, and Ittelson (1949) stress the transactional point of view in psychological research in which man is not considered as contrasted with his environment or as in action *in* a world but as man-in-action—where action means "of and by the world of which man is an integral constituent." This transactional concept differs from those of self-action and interaction in which man is considered as self-powered, or else causal interconnections are attributed to balancing systems.

Behavioral sciences are in our time alive with new vigor through the use of transactional concepts which depend on multiple frames of reference and therefore require inter-disciplinary research. The evolution of these concepts corresponds somewhat to the evolutionary complexity of the organism. Simpler forms of life processes are not abandoned but become parts of a larger whole. Simpler ways of viewing life as stages of development of science need not be abandoned but can be used in description of part functions. One can still satisfactorily view the newborn infant with its genetic constitution as a process of self-action wound up in the past like a clock and driven from behind through "instinctual drives." There is still adequacy in the description of the first "needs" of the child as it searches for the maternal warmth and succor and receives or is denied satisfaction, as a model of energy transformation and interaction, starting the primary processes of the psychological id. However, subsequent events require for an adequate description of behavior the inclusion of circular and often cyclic processes of communication among many systems small and large with a total field, all of which must be specified in time and space, including the observer. Interrelationships of phenomena such as feelings and bodily changes cannot be well understood until they are considered as operating within the transactions of multiple living foci and within the total span of experienced time with a specified environment.

Frank (1951) expresses the principles of dynamic transactions within field theory clearly as follows: "Today we are
beginning to formulate a dynamic concept of organization
which, as in embryology, is in terms of field theory. In field
theory what we call 'parts' are not to be conceived as separate, independent, randomly self-acting entities. The
'parts' are what we have selected for observation within a
dynamic organized complex; these so-called 'parts' are continually acting, reacting, interacting, *transacting,* by a reciprocal circular process, as shown in organic functioning.
By their dynamic, circular activity the 'parts' create and
maintain the 'whole' which reciprocally organizes and governs the activities of the 'parts' and thereby gives rise to
that organized 'whole,' with its dynamic circular relations
to the environing field. This dynamic circular activity of
'parts-whole' in a field is what we call 'organization,' which
is not an entity or a superior power or force or something
imposed upon parts in a dominance-submission relationship, but what arises from this circular process of the
'whole' and its 'parts.'

"We cannot pick out one of these 'parts' in an organized
'whole' and endow it with causal potency as a self-acting
agent, forgetting that this 'part' and its activity is significant
only as a participant in the 'whole' which patterns its activity. Thus, in the living organism, every cell, tissue and organ
is engaged in a continuous process of functioning that
creates and maintains the intact organism which, in turn,
governs what each cell, tissue and organ does in its special-

izing functioning, to maintain the living organism as a self-repairing, self-regulating organism."

If there is no sharp barrier between the self and not-self, what is the point of investigation? Murphy (1947) states that if the organism is not an encapsulated unit, then it may be considered and studied as a node or organizing point in a field which in itself has no strict boundary but, like an electromagnetic field, is constantly changing.

John Spiegel (1953) has attempted to review the general properties of the field, indicate some convenient nodes for study (soma, psyche, group, society, culture orientations, and universe) and portray a scheme for analysis of these nodes or systems and their transactions. "If the concept of the field is to be employed as the basis for representing the interconnections between the various aspects of human behavior, then these aspects must all occupy non-hierarchical positions within the field. But before proceeding with a detailed description of a field constructed on this principle, I would like to discuss some general characteristics which presumably describe any field simply by virtue of its being constituted as a field.

"1. The field is not a static phenomenon but consists of patterned processes representing systems of organized energy which are in motion relative to one another.

"2. In spite of the continual motion and change, the pattern of transactions among the various systems composing the field has a basic stability which can be discerned. If the pattern is observed along a spatial dimension, it appears as a structure. If it is observed along a temporal dimension, it appears as a function. In other words, the distinction between a structure in the field and a function in the field is not absolute but, rather, is relative to the position of the observer. The term pattern is inclusive of both structure and function.

"3. The field is a four-dimensional continuum. Whether processes are pictured as patterned along a spatial dimension or along a temporal dimension depends on the position of the observer.

"4. Since the field is a continuum of patterned, transactional processes, the structure-function of any one part of the field affects the structure-function of all the other parts of the field, and, therefore, of the whole field. In other words, all parts of the field are in structure-function relation with each other. This total, diffuse dependence makes it theoretically impossible to isolate and observe transactions among adjacent parts of the field while ignoring the reverberating effect of changes taking place in more remote parts of the field as a result of the very processes being observed. In actual fact, however, such observations can be made on isolated parts of the field if it is stated that the reverberating effects limit the validity of the observations being made.

"5. The structural-functional interdependence of all parts of the field makes statements describing dominance or hierarchical relations of one part of the field over another essentially meaningless. For example, if biological, psychological, and cultural events are considered to be parts of the field, then such reductive statements as 'psychological processes are derived from biological processes' or 'personality is the reflection in the individual of the prevailing cultural environment' become irrelevant. Since they are all field phenomena, the particular form that each takes will depend upon the reciprocal relations among all three. One cannot be derived from another but must be considered as having spatial and temporal coexistence.

"6. Although the field is a continuum so far as its dimensions are concerned, it is not homogeneous. The energy systems of which it is composed are differentiated from each other as foci or nodes of organization. The differentiation is discerned by the observer on the basis of criteria of integration and maintenance of a 'steady state.' The identity of the foci of organization is maintained by integrative processes which facilitate energy exchanges among the system foci at rates of exchange or equilibria which preserve the pattern or order within the system. Defense processes also occur and represent partial sacrifices of structure or function within the system foci designed to control energy exchanges resulting from strain, conflict, or incongruence which, if unchecked, would lead to disintegration or loss of order. Insofar as the system foci maintain their integration, they sustain boundaries which distinguish one from another, but the boundaries between the foci are ill-defined, incomplete and variable. The character of the boundary area depends upon the degree of order in the system resulting from transactions occurring at any particular time and place.

"It is necessary to develop a scheme for coding and decoding the kinds of information we already possess about systems and their transactions. A codification scheme of this sort can be evolved if information regarding each focus of organization is assembled along three interdependent axes:

"1. The content, substance or basic components of each system. This will be denoted as the *Constitutional Determinants* of the focus of organization

"2. Processes which maintain the structures-in-function or order of the focus of organization. These will be denoted as the *Integrative Determinants* of the foci.

"3. Traits which characterize the purpose or function of the system as a whole within the field. Such traits or attributes can not be discovered from observing the basic components of the system, or the patterned relationships of its parts, but only by observing the transactions and interrelations of the system as a whole among other systems. This axis will be denoted as the *System Determinants* of the foci."

It has become the contemporary task of biological science, advanced by the borrowing of field theory from physics, to study integration in a more sophisticated manner than as a simple relationship between parts. The use of system foci in transaction within the total field requires that more than two systems be studied simultaneously. Physiologists have been accustomed to studying modes of integration which have been outlined in the first part of this chapter: enzymatic, hormonal, nervous. Psychologists have focused on intrapsychic systems, sometimes in relationship with total or specific somatic processes or symptoms and sometimes with social or cultural processes narrowly defined as "life situations" or as "reality." Anthropologists have concerned themselves with culture as an influence on somatic or personality patterns and with social forces affecting psychological states. However, often the psychosomatic field has been sharply broken into fragments which have been then artificially correlated with other fragments far removed in space and time, in structure and function. Today we have come to realize that both the genetic and the transactional approach require for analysis and synthesis the concepts of a field theory.

Is it possible to compare the component systems of the psychosomatic-social field in order to determine their similarities and differences as foci in a transactional field? It is very difficult indeed, especially since similarities derived from homologies and analogies are often alleged to satisfy the human tendency and need to close gaps and to avoid abhorrent discontinuities. However, just as organic evolution has resulted in the emergence of the most complex forms of life from the same basic patterns of the primitive unicellule carried on by genic transmission, so too do cultural elaborations stem from biological patterns, evolved and propagated by symbolic transmission. We should expect to find many points of similarity within all living systems and their elaborations. Although hierarchies and position in phylogenetic and ontogenetic time are not significant in studying current transactional processes, we may conclude that all system determinants are derived through forces of evolution, maturation, and development from earlier, simpler forms and functions, and reveal a dynamic identity (Grinker, 1939a). Each system, however, develops its own highly specialized functions after individuation has begun.

Constitutional determinants of a system may be compared with those of other systems by the method of homologizing similarities of cause and effect when the primary forces are genic or intrinsic. With a position within the system, the observer may view its activities as an apparatus with those attributes defined on page 152. These are characteristic of the somatic constitution and the psychological constitution that we term id.

Integrative determinants may be compared by the method of analogy if the observer is outside the system or at its boundaries. Here may be observed the capacity to maintain itself against disintegration or randomness—negative entropy. Freud used the term "instinct" to indicate a borderline concept between the somatic and the mental as an abstraction which compared the integrative determinants of each. A few comparisons may be put in tabular form. (See page 164.)

System determinants or those characterizing function within a field may only be determined by simultaneous

Somatic	Psychological
Needs, and need satisfactions for homeostasis	Pleasure-pain
Irritability and motility	Anxiety-levels of consciousness
Somatic learning—vegetative net conditioning; experience with body content; self-discrimination boundaries	Reality testing
Growth	Learning
Propagation	Memory or recall

observation of three or more systems (cf. Chapter XI). The observer tries to understand the processes of communication among parts and wholes. Parts of the somatic organization communicate by means of chemical or electrical signs. Communications between whole human somatic organizations are carried on by means of symbols. Therefore, the essential characteristic of a psychological system is its function of transaction between somatic signs and interpersonal symbols. Through such a process the psychological system differentiates, grows, and propagates, and maintains its pattern against disintegrative forces. It is associated with varying degrees of awareness or consciousness and has reference to the whole of the time continuum (for that organic species and that individual) and represents a confluence of the projection of all surfaces (inner, outer, etc.).

At a higher level of abstraction, when the observer is farther removed in time and space, all living systems seem to maintain integration and homeostasis in the service of self-equilibrium and prolongation of life and species. At the same time they reveal properties of reacting and expanding with growth, specialization, division of labor, and loss of autonomy. Is this another form of homeostatic function? It seems not to be based upon frustration or stress but constitutes an inherent trend of living systems which pushes toward expansion or progression of organization. As a corollary, integration becomes looser and more susceptible to strain. Between the homeostatic and expansive trends (goal seeking and goal changing) conflicts arise, and many permutations of possible solutions develop which represent varying degrees of "health."

Perhaps it has now become clearer that observations in the psychosomatic-social field are extremely complicated if we wish to understand such processes in health and sickness. For in addition to a thorough knowledge of the genetics and development of psychosomatic unity, differentiation, and mature integration, the transactional processes among its component systems should be understood. These are silent when they function best, and they are then more difficult to study. When stressful forces succeed in straining or disintegrating parts of the field, foreboding somatic signs may be observed and, in the human being, the signal of anxiety may be experienced. These phenomena will be discussed in the next chapter.

CHAPTER ELEVEN

Anxiety and Psychosomatic Transactions

LET US assume that the human organism at some time comprises one undifferentiated functional system in transaction with its environment. Out of this are differentiated many small systems which still remain under the potential dominance of the whole, but which are linked with each other in a circular process of transaction just as the total organism is related to its environment, society and culture. Each system serves as the environment of the other. The *intrapersonal* functions may be classified into many discrete systems, but it seems logical to use five large natural divisions:

1. The enzymatic system including the hormones.
2. The organ system which includes the function of each organ or their larger confluences.
3. The nervous system.
4. The psychological system.
5. The socio-cultural system.

The living boundaries between these are ill-defined, incomplete, variable, and dependent upon the transactions occurring at any particular time and place. In fact, one might state that such boundaries correspond to living semipermeable membranes of a single cell. The integration within each system and the defenses against disintegration constitute the forces that tend to maintain a steady state.

Activity in one system is probably communicated to all others and stimulates within each of them processes which often are of such small quantity and such short duration that they are only with great difficulty measurable by our existing methods. If a stimulus which impinges on an appropriate system is of such quantity or duration that it constitutes stress, responses will be set into action which tend to return that system to a relatively steady state; but other systems will also be involved in this reaction. It may be assumed that there is no sharp threshold barrier between systems because of the continuous transaction. When a given system is strained in handling a particular stress, the minor, perhaps unmeasurable, preparatory changes in another system become intensified and apparent as another response to the initial stimulus. The integration among the systems is inherent, both in preparatory activity and in more intense reaction to stress impinging on any one of them. The integration within a single system is dependent upon its capacity to act alone without strain before a new order of action is set off within other systems.

If we use oxygen deprivation as an example of stress for

our hypothesis, a change in enzymatic functions first increases the uptake and utilization within each cell of the available oxygen. Although this reaction is only observed within one system at a given tension of oxygen, all other systems are alerted. If the integrative capacity of this system is overwhelmed, the hematopoietic system may throw out more red cells to carry the limited amount of oxygen and to increase its turnover, the peripheral vascular system changes in caliber, and the heart pumps the blood cells faster to utilize the limited oxygen tension to its fullest. Greater oxygen deprivation may stimulate the nervous system to effect changes in the rate and rhythm of breathing through the action of carbon dioxide on the medullary respiratory centers. In the meantime the psychological state of the organism is alerted—at first with minor degrees of apprehension, culminating finally in an anxiety state which prepares it for flight. If all of the previous reactions are not sufficient to decrease internal disequilibrium, total coordinated voluntary behavior may destroy its containment or move the subject to flight and into an atmosphere where oxygen tension is more suitable for its needs. If we reverse the process and use a symbolic stimulus acting at a psychological level through fear of suffocation or oxygen deprivation, the result will be an intensification of activity from one system to another until the symbolic danger is no longer present or until the organism has reacted physiologically to adjust for its fear.

From a single system which may functionally disintegrate

because of strain, to all systems and eventually to a total response, activity progressively increases to enable the organism to keep a steady internal state. The result is a multiplicity of circular and corrective processes between systems which are oriented toward stabilizing the organism and maintaining its integration. A breakdown between boundaries and an intensification of activity of another system only occurs when the strain becomes too severe. Likewise, the pattern of behavior resumes its primitive infantile total functions when the several systems which have been fractionated out of the whole are no longer able to handle the stress. From the initial effect of stress in facilitating defenses, greater quantities are disruptive by producing strain and ultimately de-differentiation. If the level of excitation reaches a certain threshold, energy may be discharged in the form of violent, aggressive striking or fighting activity or rhythmic running movements. When the differentiated systems are under strain the whole takes over and the old patterns of integration return. Thus in the service of need and the response to danger in attempting to maintain a steady inner state, aggressiveness is only a quantitative variation of activity in a system of energy exchange which functions in an effort to maintain itself.

My attempt has been to demonstrate that whether the organism reacts as a primitive whole before differentiation, or is the process of straining in an effort to handle stress, or has been disrupted by excessive stress into a de-differentiated whole, somatic and psychic systems are in a constant state of transaction with each other. Concomitance of somatic and psychological action patterns probably occur only as the result of lasting traumatic impressions made upon a total system before differentiation or as the result of current stress forcing regression to that early state.

Assuming that anxiety is subjectively experienced and reported by man as a conditioned signal of danger to the organism's internal or external equilibrium, it sets into activity adaptive mechanisms of defense appropriate to the stimulus or stress. If anxiety is mild it is stimulating and facilitative to increased and efficient action or thought. If it becomes too intense, disruptive effects ensue, calling forth emergency substitutive mechanisms of defense or, in greater degrees, de-differentiated regressive behavior. Accompanying all those defenses which cannot allay anxiety through psychological mechanisms and volitional action, internal vegetative organ functions become increased and overt as parts of the "fight-flight" mechanisms—or, to put it in another way, as manifestations of more primitive undifferentiated psychosomatic responses which are called upon to replace the unsuccessful psychological maneuvers. Thus, a study of free anxiety becomes basic to the problem of psychosomatic disturbances. We should like to know the stresses which evoke anxiety—somatic by internal signs, or environmental by interpersonal symbols, or both at the same time. We want to know the somatic accompaniments and the short- or long-term somatic results of anxiety. The latter have assumed significance since army experience has

taught us that severe long-standing anxiety can stir up reverberating somatic effects which persist long after the anxiety
itself has disappeared.

Our preliminary research showed that liver function is a
sensitive indicator of the presence of free anxiety, especially in its function in hippuric acid synthesis. We have
shown that anxiety-free catatonic schizophrenics and
anxiety-ridden persons constitute the opposite ends of a
theoretical gradient and that hippuric acid excretion is a
quantitative index of an individual's position in the gradient (Persky *et al.*, 1950a, 1950b, 1952). Of particular significance is the fact that it is "free anxiety"—which in time
and quantity becomes unendurable and provokes the symptoms of psychoneuroses or psychoses as defenses—that can
be correlated wth biochemical changes such as hippuric
acid synthesis. This synthesis is probably only one of the
many biochemical and hormonal processes which respond
to changes in the degree of basic psychological tension or
anxiety. It is in this early phase of free anxiety, rather than
later, when defensive neurotic or psychotic symptoms or
behavior have developed, that related psychological and
physiological (biochemical) processes activate patterns
which become specific.

The neural or endocrine mechanisms involved in this and
other processes of basic psychosomatic relatedness can be
identified. The signal acting in this mechanism must enter
the receptor system and be perceived as meaningful to the
organism. Our studies have indicated that laboratory sit-

uations are in themselves not sufficiently charged with danger to mobilize pathological anxiety or biochemical changes of appreciable quantity. The stimulus must be perceived in the light of inner expectation, originating at an early and particularly helpless time in the organism's history, to be dangerous to its protective attachments and hence to its existence. A particular organism has failed, or has never had the opportunity, to learn that changed reality, its lessened needs and its greater adaptability, make the stimulus less dangerous or entirely innocuous. Thus, disturbed with intense free anxiety it must take flight. But at this first period it is in a state of fluid emergent mobilization: of anxiety, paralleled by the liberation of many yet undetermined biochemical products.

Some individuals stay in this state of "free anxiety," which is truly delay or paralysis (neither fight nor flight) for a considerable time. Some are able to attack the stimulus aggressively and overcome its disturbance (fight). Others choose to fly either into psychological avoidance, conversion, or manipulation of the anxiety into a psychoneurotic defense system, or withdraw from the scene into a catatonic stupor. War neuroses demonstrated the rapid waxing and waning of free anxiety with these types of flights. In either category of events, anxiety diminishes or disappears and the biochemical process slows down. The psychoneurotic never retreats quite far enough or successfully enough. His defenses are always under fire and eventually have to give way. Hence his biochemical processes, using hippuric acid excretion as an example, are more like those of the normally apprehensive person. The catatonic hibernates and, like such an inactive animal, has a hippuric acid excretion far below normal values.

The question may be raised whether biochemical changes are restricted to patients with severe anxiety or panic, or whether they exist, though perhaps in lesser degree, in subjects with less anxiety and in essentially healthy individuals facing severe but temporary stress in a life situation. In exploring this problem, studies were conducted on university graduate students facing examinations and on patients with anxiety freed by sodium pentothal and hypnosis. Although hippuric acid excretion is not raised to the level found in patients with free anxiety, there is some evidence for a distinct and perhaps significant elevation. Thus, it seems possible that hippuric acid excretion may provide a continuous measure of degree of anxiety. The logical next step, therefore, was to study healthy subjects during a period of stress in a real life situation (paratrooper training), in which anxiety in varying degrees may be expected to be aroused, handled, and allayed, at various levels of functioning, biochemical, psychiatric, and psychological, and to integrate the findings into a more comprehensive picture. In such research it is important to study *simultaneously* (as far as possible) various aspects of the total organism's response, manifested at different levels of function and through different systems, and to make such measurements while the organism is in the *process* of responding in the life situation. With such an approach, laws of organismic functioning in, let us say, the stress situation can in time be developed—laws which describe the continuities and relations among systems, in their stable states and in change. This conception of psychosomatic research is essentially different from the more traditional, in which persons in terminal disintegrative states of one system—for example, a somatic disease which is an end point—are studied (Korchin, Persky, Basowitz, Grinker, 1953).

Although free anxiety is a subjective and reportable feeling and by this definition is essentially human, other animals show evidence of anxiety in their behavior, states of tension, somatic regressions, and chronic disorders of many organs. In the phylogenetic series of evolution before and beyond the human individual, evidences of homologous conditions exist. Manifestations of anxiety within groups and societies, in forms spoken of as social or cultural tensions, are reported by anthropologists and other social scientists. Irritability, tension states, and vigilance are spoken of by biologists and animal psychologists. There is thus not only an ontogeny, but also a phylogeny of anxiety.

An investigation of anxiety always evokes the problem of the differentiation between *stimulus,* which is needed by the organism to set in action or to keep activated its life processes, and *stress,* which threatens or unduly disturbs the organism's equilibrium. Stress is a relative concept depending, not on its absolute measurement or duration, but on the state of the organism, the time at which it is disturbed, its past experience, its capacity in reference to its age, and the functional capacities in the field in which the organism or its part exists at the moment. The single-celled animal may react with increased and random movements, ultimate massing into groups, encapsulation, rapid storage of food products, or sexual reproduction and spore formation. Multicellular animals have the capacity for more rapid communication through nerve nets, primitive learning by conditioning, and hormonal production of acetylcholine and adrenalin.

These prototypes of anxiety have a cost for the organism. Communication and motility are reduced, greater sources of energy-producing substances are needed, and there is a reduction of individual growth. Stimuli may be considered as sources of growth and adaptation, and eventually learning and evolution. Stress is responsible for costly adaptive changes for the organism. Within the highest psychological functions, stress stirs up defensive maneuvers which cost energy and deplete the ego's functions for productive activity and new learning, plus the general somatic regressive activity.

Stress may result in passive diminution of contact with the environment, active escape from, or struggle with, the environment, or active change in internal regulation. The effects upon the organism may facilitate integrative capacities, stir up defenses against disintegration, or finally result in disintegration. These need to be defined in time and in transaction with the environment. The birth of anxiety occurs at the moment of beginning transaction between organism and environment, anthropomorphized as the point of uncertainty when action has not yet started or has failed.

Having arrived at the conclusion that irritability is the fundamental function out of which the specter of human anxiety has evolved, we may now attempt to define it. Irritability is a property of all living protoplasm; hence it is concomitant with life—accentuated and intensified, however, in specialized tissues such as the nervous system, which has the capacity to detonate explosively and conduct speedily (Toman and Taylor, 1952). We may define irritability as a property of living substances that depends for evocation upon stimuli (internal or external to the organism) and which manifests itself by change in quantity, tempo, or direction of its previous state.

As C. J. Herrick (1930) says, "Life is a system of forces maintained by energy exchange between the system and its environment, correlated to conserve the identity of the system as an individual and to propagate it as a species." Irritability is, therefore, that state that enables the organism (in man, his organs and his organ systems) to recognize and accept stimuli and to respond with appropriate conserving and propagating action. Such action will effect change temporarily, since there is a force of inertia and a tendency to revert toward the previous state of equilibrium unless other aspects of the system follow the change, which then becomes incorporated as a permanent state, corresponding to the phenomena of growth, learning, adjustment, and evolution. Generally, then, irritability is the state of readiness for change or response and may be considered as partly genic, partly acquired, with variable forms within different living systems and at different times within the same system. We may take the liberty of using the term "irritability" as generic to identify a basic protoplasmic property, threshold attributes of living systems, behavioral vigilance, and psychological anxiety. I have chosen to emphasize the relationship of protoplasmic irritability and psychological anxiety since psychosomatic research is so vitally concerned with internal somatic processes which are set into action by psychological anxiety through the biological homologue of anxiety-irritability.

Anxiety is a process that has been weighed and measured by psychiatrists on a negative balance, for they have observed, described, and analyzed defenses which when removed would liberate bound, repressed, or converted anxiety, or its short-circuited energy. We have been accustomed for too long to the operations by which anxiety is measured by its physiological climaxes and side-chains or by its influences on ego functions—facilitating or activating them, stirring up their defenses, or destroying their effectiveness. The psychosomatic aspects of anxiety can really be better understood if we consider that aspect of it which is "free"— consciously experienced, suffered, and self-reported. Since the human psyche finds this the most unendurable state, free anxiety rarely exists for long, being rapidly repressed or bound by defenses, except in the severe examples of traumatic and war neuroses.

Most psychologists and psychiatrists have sought for a somatic hypothesis for the derivation and meaning of anxiety. Freud (1936) tackled the problem most seriously, for he recognized that this phenomenon was the central focus of a dynamic psychiatry. He first considered it as a direct transmutation from dammed-up libido, thereby implicitly indicating a somatic source. He later toyed with the idea that its cause was the trauma of birth rather than its first integrated somatic expression, the intensity of which may forecast the later developing ego's integrative capacity. Finally he conceived anxiety as a signal experienced by the self or ego, always present as a continuous anticipation of inner or outer danger and pathologically present as a signal of continuous internalized psychological danger which the organism cannot avoid by the customary procedures of aggressively attacking or passively fleeing.

The refinement of anxiety as a signal developed as the distant receptors evolved, especially that of olfaction, for this enabled the organism to project itself in future time and anticipate far ahead the satisfaction of needs or the presence of danger (Grinker, 1939a). The great forces by which sensory systems activate the cerebral cortex (MacLean, 1949; Kubie, 1953b) particularly affect the rhinencephalon or visceral brain which Herrick long ago stated exerts a tonic effect or learning pressure on the cerebral cortex. It is this primarily olfactory and secondarily visceral brain which, standing between inner signs of need or pressure (the "I") and outer social symbols of safety and satisfaction (the "not I"), seems most vitally concerned in the development of the anxiety signal.

Human anxiety, therefore, is a subjective signal which develops when self has become an entity. The undifferentiated organism or the part organs may demonstrate irritability, vigilance, and reactive startle, but not anxiety. When the self as a distinct body and psychological ego has matured, it may then be projected into future time and space, and experience the signal of anxiety, which constantly feeds an alerting process into the composite psychosomatic organization. Anxiety is a psychological function, for it only appears when time for psychological action is available. Reflex action, immediate automatic behavior without delay, are not associated with anxiety; in fact, they are defenses against this affect. What is necessary is an awareness of need or binding of action in a state of delay. The result may be the initiation of accelerated, quantitative, or directional changes in local or total behavior, or anxiety may be the source of defenses against the subjective state itself.

The defenses against anxiety itself are developed when there is failure to alleviate the need or to avoid the danger when anxiety has been stirred by it. Needs and dangers which are interpreted as real by his society permit man to make preparation for action and usually more or less appropriate behavior. When the social environment denies the reality of stress and forbids certain defensive actions, threats must be internalized and are felt as anxiety. Since anxiety is a signal of internally symbolized anachronistic dangers or frustrations, it is self-perpetuating, since no action can pull or push a man away from what is in him. As a result the subjective signal itself becomes a danger which "feeds upon itself"—spirals in accelerated increase—unless defensive processes are set into action. These processes are partly in the realm of fantasy, behavior, and regression. All of them in some manner deny existing reality, interfere with ego functions, and involve the entire psychosomatic organization in the process of rechannelizing energy (Thetford, 1952). Although adaptive to the stress, the adjustment secondarily becomes disease.

Multiple psychosomatic systems respond to alleviate need, overcome obstacles, or adjust to frustration. They prepare for or participate in emergency action and disintegrate functionally if the anxiety and the called-for responses of excessive alertness or action persist in time or extend in quantity. These processes are always transactional among many systems which represent nodes created by the focus of the observer and may be larger or smaller depending on the awareness of the techniques utilized. For an analysis of transactional processes three or more systems must be utilized (Thompson, 1951, 1952), although most psychosomatic research dealing with relationships, concomitant or regressive, utilizes only two systems. In transactional analysis the system stimulated or stressed in need or in danger is in the fovea of the field. Its immediate environment consists of the system or systems feeding into it (its sources of input) and the system or systems affected by it (its targets of output). The influence of stress on a system makes it function like a stone thrown into the water. The target is violently disturbed, and from it ripples of effect gradually spread in a circle with decreasing intensity and speed at the periphery.

Other systems respond as internal emergency mechanisms, intensifying input or substituting for output—what we call compensatory or, in some cases, vicarious functioning. They may exist in multiple chains as secondary, tertiary, etc., emergency mechanisms. Still other systems prepare or react for emergency behavior directly attacking or changing the external environment or altering the organism's position within it. It may be surmised that the internal emergency mechanisms are affected by parasympathetic anabolic functions and by sympathetic and voluntary nervous discharge. All are in concomitant, reciprocal, and successive action, and psychosomatic function may not be logically classified according to the artificial divisions of nervous system as to size of fibers, enzyme utilization, source of outflow, phylogeny, or ontogeny. Finally, some systems disintegrate under stress, becoming secondary stimuli to further internal adjustment and compensation. It seems probable that the causal chain of processes involved in disease (defense, regression) are linked to the functions of the emergency systems and the disintegrating processes.

Since etiology is not a linear cause and effect, a direct and monistic relationship between graded hierarchical levels of complexity, we should study circular, transactional, and corrective processes with the greatest effort toward inclusiveness; at least, excluded processes should be defined. In any case, the observer's position, his focus, and the extent of the environment of the focus to be studied should be clearly stated. Its social and cultural aspects should be included by implication or preferably by specification, since there is no workable psychosomatic hypothesis which does not include social and cultural influences as participants in development, function, stress, and strain. Life processes occur, at all levels of development, with varying participation of all systems depending on the stage of undifferentiation, differentiation, or de-differentiation, on the number of consecutive or concomitant tasks, on the presence of unusual types, quantity, repetitiveness, or prolongation of strain.

We may now make several assumptions:

1. The internal properties (constitution) of a system are measurable or at least comparable to those of other systems.

2. A system's capacities for maintaining integration, when under type, quantity, and time of stresses which strain a system beyond its maintenance functions, can be measured or compared.

3. Transactional relations with other systems and the changes in them when a system is strained, can be measured or at least observed.

4. The threshold for the processes in and the results of disintegration of a system can be measured.

From transactions resulting in intensified integrative processes (2), or in disintegration (4), profound variations in 3 may be expected. Although we cannot predict the degree or direction of results of 3, since they probably vary with the properties of the stress and the state of the transacting systems, the general patterns can be observed. From these we may draw conclusions as to the specificity of processes in relation to known variables and develop hypotheses and create experimental designs for their testing.

A general plan can be indicated for the development of these hypotheses. System relationships should be studied when not strained as a base-line record of pre-stress. Stress may then be applied (for example, hypoxia) which cannot be specific for a single system, since no system can be isolated in the intact human, and the spreading effects are just those that we want to observe. The stress should be applied in varying degrees, from a quantity which strains to one that disintegrates (to a safe end point).

The following phenomena may be taken into account:

1. The effect of stress on all systems, especially the one most sensitive to the point of disintegration of function. The word "all" here applies to all those under study in a particular experiment, depending on the techniques or investigative disciplines available for the research.

2. Observations as nearly simultaneous as possible on the

timing of change, on its degree, and on the directions of input and output systems closely related to the focus of stress. Without an approach to simultaneity transactional process cannot be clearly understood.

3. Observations on emergency mechanisms.

4. Observations on behavior-alerting mechanisms, especially anxiety at the psychological level.

5. Observations on the total action, its delay, and the somatic changes occurring with it.

6. Observations on the psychological processes defending against perception of stress, action, and anxiety.

The operational procedures for research into transactional processes relative to psychosomatic problems are extremely complicated. They require the assumption that "psychosomatic" refers to dynamic processes dependent upon the functions (in the mathematical sense) of many cyclic part processes. We should be able to set up a model of this organization applicable to the analysis of the states of anxiety, depression, consciousness, etc.

Through adequate statistical operations anxiety may be studied as a transactional process among several sytsems closest to the central nervous system and empirically known to be significant "functions" of anxiety. Relations between peripheral foci and the central system, relations among themselves, and reciprocal alteration in cycles may be observed. The model poses many difficulties in adequate experimental operations of interference and measurements especially in the field of ego transactions, but at least first attempts can be made.

From the above we may obtain a knowledge of the deepest somatic processes from somatic responsiveness characterizing irritability to the psychological signal of anxiety, and the steps by which the psychological level is reached, the input systems, the concomitants of anxiety, the output or effects of anxiety, and the psychologically facilitating and destructive effects of anxiety. Such research will greatly amplify our knowledge of psychosomatic processes in health and illness.

Since this book was written, we have been engaged in considerable research on psychophysiological relationships utilizing anxiety as our focus. We embarked on this program with the idea that psychosomatic correlations in specific diseases were premature and had led to spurious conclusions; that, first, greater knowledge of the general laws of psycho-physiology should be acquired. Below is a partial bibliography of our own investigations, in chronological order:

1. Basowitz, H., Persky, H., Korchin, S. J., and Grinker, R. R.: *Anxiety and Stress.* McGraw-Hill Book Company, Inc., New York, 1955.
2. Jeans, R., and Toman, J. E. P.: "Anxiety and Cerebral Excitability." *Archives of Neurology and Psychiatry,* 75:534, 1956.

3. Basowitz, H., Korchin, S., Oken, D., Goldstein, M., and Gussack, H.: "Anxiety and Performance Changes with a Minimal Dose of Epinephrine." *A.M.A. Archives of Neurology and Psychiatry,* 76:98, 1956.

4. Board, F., Persky, H., and Hamburg, D.: "Psychological Stress and Endocrine Functions." *Psychosomatic Medicine,* 18:4, 1956.

5. Grinker, R., Korchin, S., Basowitz, H., Hamburg, D., Sabshin, M., Persky, H., Chevalier, J., and Board, F.: "A Theoretical and Experimental Approach to Problems of Anxiety." *A.M.A. Archives of Neurology and Psychiatry,* 76:420, 1956.

6. Grinker, R. R.: "Psychosomatic Approach to Anxiety." *American Journal of Psychiatry,* 113:5, 1956.

7. Persky, H., Grinker, R., Hamburg, D., Sabshin, M., Korchin, S., Basowitz, H., and Chevalier, J.: "Adrenal Cortical Functioning in Anxious Human Subjects." *A.M.A. Archives of Neurology and Psychiatry,* 76:549, 1956.

8. Grinker, R. R., Sabshin, M., Hamburg, D. A., Board, F. A., Basowitz, H., Korchin, S. J., Persky, H., and Chevalier, J. "The Use of an Anxiety-Producing Interview and Its Meaning to the Subject." *A.M.A. Archives of Neurology and Psychiatry,* 77:406, 1957.

9. Glickstein, M., Chevalier, J. A., Korchin, S. J., Basowitz, H., Sabshin, M., Hamburg, D. A., and Grinker, R. R.: "Temporal Heart Rate Patterns in Anxious

Patients." *A.M.A. Archives of Neurology and Psychiatry,* 78:101, 1957.

10. Sabshin, M., Hamburg, D. A., Grinker, R. R., Persky, H., Basowitz, H., Korchin, S. J., and Chevalier, J. A.: "Significance of Preexperimental Studies in the Psychosomatic Laboratory." *A.M.A. Archives of Neurology and Psychiatry,* 78:207, 1957.

11. Persky, H.: "Adrenocortical Function in Anxious Human Subjects: The Disappearance of Hydrocortisone from Plasma and Its Metabolic Fate." *Journal of Clinical Endocrinology and Metabolism,* 17:760, 1957.

12. Korchin, S. J., Basowitz, H., Chevalier, J. A., Grinker, R. R., Hamburg, D. A., Sabshin, M., and Persky, H.: "Visual Discrimination and the Decision Process in Anxiety." *A.M.A. Archives of Neurology and Psychiatry,* 78:425, 1957.

13. Board, F., Wadeson, R., and Persky, H.: "Depressive Affect and Endocrine Function." *A.M.A. Archives of Neurology and Psychiatry,* 78:612, 1957.

14. Hamburg, D. A., Sabshin, M., Board, F. A., Grinker, R. R., Korchin, S. J., Basowitz, H., Heath, H., and Persky, H.: "Classification and Rating of Emotional Experiences." *A.M.A. Archives of Neurology and Psychiatry,* 79:415, 1958.

15. Persky, H., Hamburg, D. A., Basowitz, H., Grinker, R. R., Sabshin, M., Korchin, S. J., Herz, M., Board,

F. A., and Heath, H.: "Relation of Emotional Responses and Changes in Plasma Hydrocortisone Level after Stressful Interview." *A.M.A. Archives of Neurology and Psychiatry,* 79:434, 1958.

16. Korchin, S. J., Basowitz, H., Grinker, R. R., Hamburg, D. A., Persky, H., Sabshin, M., Heath, H., and Board, F. A.: "Experience of Perceptual Distortion As a Source of Anxiety." *A.M.A. Archives of Neurology and Psychiatry,* 80:98, 1958.

17. Persky, H., Korchin, S. J., Basowitz, H., Board, F. A., Sabshin, M., Hamburg, D. A., and Grinker, R. R.: "Effect of Two Psychological Stresses on Adrenocortical Function." *A.M.A. Archives of Neurology and Psychiatry,* 81:219, 1959.

18. Grinker, R. R.: "Anxiety as a Significant Variable for a Unified Theory of Human Behavior." *A.M.A. Archives of General Psychiatry,* 1:537, 1959.

19. Glickstein, M.: "Temporal Patterns of Cardiovascular Response." *A.M.A. Archives of General Psychiatry,* 2:12, 1960.

20. Schwartz, N. B., and Kling, A.: "Stress-Induced Adrenal Ascorbic Acid Depletion in the Cat." *Endocrinology,* Vol. 6, No. 2, Feb. 1960, pp. 308-310.

21. Engel, B. T.: "Stimulus-Response and Individual-Response Specificity. *A.M.A. Archives of General Psychiatry,* 2:305, 1960.

22. Oken, D.: "An Experimental Study of Suppressed Anger and Blood Pressure." *A.M.A. Archives of*

General Psychiatry, 2:441, 1960.

23. Korchin, S. J., and Herz, M.: "Differential Effects of Shame and Disintegrative Threats on Emotional and Adrenocortical Functioning." *A.M.A. Archives of General Psychiatry,* 2:640, 1960.

24. Oken, D., Grinker, R. R., Heath, H. A., Sabshin, M., and Schwartz, N.: "Stress Response in a Group of Chronic Psychiatric Patients with Special Reference to the Use of Curare as a Stressful Stimulus." *Archives of General Psychiatry,* 1960.

25. Heath, H. A., Oken, D., Korchin, S. J., and Towne, J. C.: A factor analytic study of multivariate psychosomatic changes over time. *Arch. Gen. Psychiat.,* 3:467, 1960.

26. Korchin, S. J., and Heath, H. A.: Somatic experience in the anxiety state. *J. Consult. Psychol.,* 25:398, 1961.

27. Blatt, S.: Patterns of cardiac arousal during complex cognitive activity. *J. Abnorm. & Soc. Psychol.,* 63:272, 1961.

28. Oken, D., Grinker, R. R., Heath, H. A., Herz, M., Korchin, S. J., Sabshin, M., Schwartz, N. B.: Relation of physiological response to affect expression. *Arch. Gen. Psychiat.,* 5:336, 1962.

29. Oken, D.: "The Role of Defense in Psychological Stress." In Roessler and Greenfield (eds.): *Physiological Correlates of Psychological Disorder.* University of Wisconsin Press, Madison, Wisconsin, 1962.

30. Heath, H. A. and Oken, D.: Change scores as related to

initial and final levels. *Annals of the New York Acad. of Sciences,* 98:1242, 1962.

31. Oken, D. and Heath, H. A.: The law of initial values: some further considerations. *Psychosom. Med.* 25:3, 1963.

32. Goldstein, I.: Physiological responses in anxious women patients. *Arch. Gen. Psych.,* 10:382, 1964.

33. Goldstein, I. B.: Role of muscle tension in personality theory. *Psychol. Bull.,* Vol. 6, 413-425.

34. Goldstein, I. B., Grinker, R. R., Sr., Heath, H. A., Oken, D., and Shipman, W. G.: Study in psychophysiology of muscle tension I response specificity. *Arch. Gen. Psych.,* 11:322, 1964.

35. Goldstein, I. B.: The relationship of muscle tension and autonomic activity to psychiatric disorders. *Psychosom. Med.,* 27:39, 1965.

36. Heath, H. A. and Oken, D.: The quantification of response to experimental stimuli. *Psychosom. Med.,* 27:457, 1965.

37. Grinker, R. R., Sr.: "Psychosomatic Aspects of the Cancer Problem." In Bahnson and Kissen (eds.): *Psychophysiological Aspects of Cancer. Annals of New York Acad. Med.,* 125:876-883, 1966.

38. Grinker, R. R., Sr.: "The Psychosomatic Aspects of Anxiety." In Spielberger (ed): *Anxiety and Behavior.* Academic Press, New York, 1966.

39. Heath, H. A.: The specificity of response to stress stimuli, with Oken, D., Shipman, W. G., Goldstein, I.,

Grinker, R. R., Sr., and Fisch, J. *Arch. Gen. Psychiat.*, 15:624, 1966.

40. Grinker, R. R., Sr.: "Psychoanalysis and the Study of Autonomic Behavior." In Rogow (ed.): *Politics, Personality and Social Science in the Twentieth Century.* University of Chicago Press, Chicago, 1969.

41. Shipman, W. G., Ph.D.: Muscle tension and effort at self-control during anxiety, with Heath, H. A. and Oken, D. *Arch. Gen. Psych.*, 23:359-368, 1970.

42. Shipman, W. G., Ph.D.: Response specificity among muscular and autonomic variables, with Heath, H. A. and Oken, D. *Arch. Gen. Psych.*, 23:369-374, 1970.

CHAPTER TWELVE

Conclusions

A CRITICAL analysis of existing theories and hypotheses of any field of science becomes necessary from time to time to counteract complacency and stimulate thinking. This has for some time been needed in the field of psychosomatic medicine, which, as its name implies, has been concerned with the sick, although psychosomatic principles have not even been well formulated, a coherent body of knowledge has not been successfully compiled, nor operational procedures developed. Diagnoses, in the meantime, are hastily arrived at on the basis of shadowy specific stereotypes, and rapid or brief methods of therapy have been advocated, even for the unskilled, to be applied to the most deep-seated and recalcitrant chronic dysfunctions, and to rigid psychological defenses.

"Psychosomatic" connotes more than a kind of illness; it is a comprehensive approach to the totality of an integrated process of transactions among many systems: somatic, psychic, social, and cultural. It deals with a living process that is born, matures, and develops through differentiation and successive stages of new forms of integration of parts and other wholes. It deals with stresses, strains, and adjustments, with acute emergency mechanisms, disintegrations, and chronic defensive states or disease. In fact, "psychosomatic" refers not to physiology or pathophysiology, not to psychology or psychopathology, but to a concept of process among all living systems and their social and cultural elaborations.

As one considers these transactional processes it becomes clear that no further refinement in the biological or social sciences or in the psychological disciplines is necessary to begin the development of sound psychosomatic concepts. Whatever is available as adequate hypotheses in any field, whatever tools of observation and measurement can be used by any discipline, are suitable to further psychosomatic understanding providing that the organismic-environmental transactional field is not dichotomized.

It has often occurred to me that we would have fared better if we had used the term "behavioral science," which implies psychosomatic or comprehensive approaches. It deals with man as a biological organism striving as part of his animal, human, and physical environment for continuity and for self-fulfillment as an individual, as he integrates into varying-sized groups. It deals with the vicissitudes of his struggle between his inner energies, their quantitative and economic aspects, and the forces conducive and antagonistic to their discharge or satisfactions. The evolution of these forces and their internal signs, with their satisfactions and dangers, into socially communicable symbols and the evolution of irritability into vigilance and consciously experienced anxiety, has led to the process of symbolic internalization of danger and intrapsychic defenses. As a result the acute emergency responses to external danger are less disturbing to man than the long continuous psychosomatic reactions to stresses that have become internalized and cannot be avoided or abandoned. "Basic psychiatry" or comprehensive medicine becomes focused on anxiety—its source, processes and effects—as a continuous function in man. Health and illness vary only in degree of smoothness of transactional operations, in nearness to equilibrium or disintegration, and degree of de-differentiation in response to stress, signaled by anxiety.

The focus of research in this field loses rather than gains sharpness when artificially simple correlations or interrelations are chosen for analysis. Freud was able long ago to recognize this fact, and if one reinterprets his writings, to be sure in the light of what we now know, his blueprint for "the future of medicine" was already laid down in principle long before the term "psychosomatic" was prematurely formalized. I do not advocate that we remain satisfied with such generalizations, but that on a basis of valid empirically derived assumptions we proceed with logical hypotheses into the fields of observational and experimental research of genetic and transactional processes.

Bibliography

Abraham, K.: *Selected Papers on Psychoanalysis* (Chapters 24, 26). Hogarth Press, London, 1927.

Adler, A.: *The Practice and Theory of Individual Psychology.* Harcourt, Brace, New York, 1924. Translation from original of 1912.

Adrian, E. C.: "Conduction in Peripheral Nerve and in the Central Nervous System." *Brain,* 41:23, 1918.

Alexander, F.: "The Logic of Emotions and Its Dynamic Background." *Int. Journ. Psychoa.,* 16:399, 1935.

————: *The Medical Value of Psychoanalysis.* Norton, New York, 1936.

————: *Psychosomatic Medicine.* Norton, New York, 1950.

Alexander, F., and French, T.: *Studies in Psychosomatic Medicine.* Ronald Press, New York, 1948.

Alkan, L.: *Anatomische Organkrankheiten aus Seelischer Ursache.* Hippokrates Verlag, Stuttgart, 1930.

Anderson, O. D., and Liddell, H. S.: "Observations on Experimental Neuroses in Sheep." *Arch. Neurol. & Psych.,* 34:330, 1935.

Arieti, S.: "Primitive Habits and Perceptual Alterations in the Terminal Stages of Schizophrenia." *Arch. Neurol. & Psych.,* 66:1, 1943.

Babkin, B., and Van Buren, J. M.: "Mechanism and Cortical Representation of the Feeding Pattern." A.M.A., *Arch. Neurol. & Psych.*, 66:1, 1951.

Bechterew, W. von: *Die Funktionen der Nervencentra.* G. Fischer, Jena, 1908–1911, 3 volumes.

Benedek, T.: "The Psychosomatic Implications of the Primary Unit: Mother-Child." *Amer. Journ. Orthopsych.*, 19:642, 1949.

———: "Personality Development." Chapter IV in *Dynamic Psychiatry,* edited by Alexander and Ross. University of Chicago Press, 1952 (a).

———: *Psychosexual Functions in Women.* Ronald Press, New York, 1952 (b).

———: "On the Organization of Psychic Energy: Instincts, Drives and Affects." Chapter V in Grinker, *Mid-Century Psychiatry.* Thomas, Springfield, 1953.

Bentley, A. F.: "Kennetic Inquiry." *Science,* 112:775, 1950.

Bergman, G. von: "Ulcus Duodeni und Vegetatives Nervensystem." *Berliner-Klin. Wochenschr.,* 50:710, 1913.

Bernard, C.: *An Introduction to the Study of Experimental Medicine.* Macmillan, New York, 1927 (1865).

Bertalanffy, L.: "The Theory of Open Systems in Physics and Biology." *Science,* 111:23, 1950.

Binger, C.: "On So-Called Psychogenic Influences in Essential Hypertension." *Psychosom. Med.,* 13:273, 1951.

Brodal, A.: "The Hippocampus and the Sense of Smell." *Brain,* 70:179, 1947.

Cannon, W. B.: *The Wisdom of the Body.* Norton, New York, 1932.

Cantril, H., Ames, A., Hastorf, A. H., and Ittelson, W. H.: "Psychology and Scientific Research." *Science,* 110:461, 491, 517, 1949.

Carmichael, L.: *Manual of Child Psychology.* Wiley, New York, 1946.

Caudill, Wm.: *Applied Anthropology in Medicine in "An Inventory of Modern Anthropology."* Werner-Glenn Foundation, 1953.

Chavoor, A. G.: "Psychosomatic Factors in Oral Disease." *Bulletin of U.S. Army Medical Department,* 9:987, 1949.

Child, C. M.: *The Organ and Development of the Nervous System from a Physiological Viewpoint.* University of Chicago Press, 1921.

Cooper, L. F.: "Time Distortion in Hypnosis." *Journ. of Psychology,* 34:257, 1952.

Corner, G. W.: *Ourselves Unborn.* Yale University Press, New Haven, 1944.

Cushing, H.: *Pituitary Body and Hypothalamus.* Thomas, Springfield, 1932.

Darwin, C.: *The Expression of the Emotions in Man and Animals.* D. Appleton, New York, 1897.

————: *The Descent of Man and Selection in Relation to Sex.* D. Appleton, New York, 1871.

Deutsch, F.: "Der Gesunde und der Kranke Körper in Psychoanalytischer Betrachtung." *Int. Zeit. of Psa.,* 8:290, 1922.

————: "Thus Speaks the Body." *Transact. New York Acad. Med.,* 12:2, 1949.

————: "Thus Speaks the Body." *Acta Medica Orientalia,* 9: 199, 1950 and 10:67, 1951.

————: "Analytic Posturology." *Psychoanalytic Quarterly,* 21:196, 1952.

Dewey, J.: *Problems of Men*. Philosophical Library, New York, 1946.

Draper, G.: *Human Constitution: A Consideration of Its Relationship to Disease*. Saunders, Philadelphia, 1924.

Dunbar, H. F.: *Emotions and Bodily Changes*. Columbia University Press, New York, 1935.

————: *Psychosomatic Diagnosis*. Hoeber, New York, 1943.

Edinger, L.: "Ueber die dem Oralsinne dienenden apparate am Gehirn der Sauger." Vogel, Leipzig, 1908.

Engel, G.: "Homeostasis, Behavioral Adjustment and the Concept of Health and Disease." Chapter IV in Grinker, *Mid-Century Psychiatry*. Thomas, Springfield, 1953.

Erikson, E. H.: *Childhood and Society*. Norton, New York, 1950.

Farquharson, R. F.: *Simmonds' Disease*. Thomas, Springfield, 1950.

Ferenczi, S.: *Sex in Psychoanalysis* (collected papers). Basic Books, New York, 1950.

Frank, L. K.: "Genetic Psychology and Its Prospects." *Amer. Journ. Orthopsych.*, 21:506, 1951.

Frazer, J. G.: *The Golden Bough, A Study in Magic and Religion*. Third Edition, Macmillan, New York, 1935.

French, T.: "Physiology of Behavior and Choice of Neurosis." *Psychoanalytic Quarterly*, 10:561, 1941.

————: *Integrative Behavior*. University of Chicago Press, 1952.

Freud, S.: *Three Contributions to the Sexual Theory*. Nervous and Mental Disease Monographs, New York, 1910.

————: *The Problem of Anxiety*. Norton, New York, 1936.

————: *Gesammelte Werke*. 14 volumes. Imago Press, London —various dates.

————: *Collected Papers*. Hogarth Press, London, 5 volumes— various dates.

Fries, M.: "Factors in Character Development, Neuroses, Psychoses and Delinquency." *Amer. Journ. Ortho.,* 7:142, 1937.

————: "Psychosomatic Relationship between Mother and Infant." *Psychosom. Med.,* 6:159, 1944.

Fulton, J. F.: *Physiology of the Nervous System.* Oxford Med. Pub., New York, 1938.

Gesell, A.: "Morphologies of Mouth and Mouth Behavior." *Amer. Journ. of Orthodontics and Oral Surgery,* 28:397, 1942.

Gesell, A., and Ilg, F. L.: *Feeding Behavior of Infants.* Lippincott, New York, 1937.

————: *Vision: Its Development in Infant and Child.* Hoeber, New York, 1939.

Gesell, A., and Armatruda, C. S.: *Developmental Diagnosis.* Hoeber, New York, 1941.

Glover, E.: "The Significance of the Mouth in Psychoanalysis." *British Journ. Med. Psychol.,* 4:134, 1924.

————: "Examination of the Klein System of Child Psychology." *The Psychoanalytic Study of the Child,* 1:75, 1945.

Grace, Wm., Wolf, S., and Wolff, H.: *The Human Colon.* Hoeber, New York, 1951.

Greenacre, P.: "The Biological Economy of Birth." *The Psychoanalytic Study of the Child,* 1:31, 1945.

————: *Trauma, Growth and Personality.* W. W. Norton, New York, 1952.

Gregory, Wm. K.: *Our Face from Fish to Man.* Putnam, New York, 1929.

Grinker, R. R.: "Elektrische Reizung der Basal Ganglien bei

einem Falle von Anankephalie." *Zeitschr. f.d. gesamte Neurol. u. Psych.*, 135:573, 1931.

Grinker, R. R.: *Neurology*. First Edition, Thomas, Springfield, 1934.

———: "A Comparison of 'Psychological Repression' and Neurological 'Inhibition.'" *Journ. Nerv. & Ment. Dis.*, 89:765, 1939 (a).

———: "Hypothalamic Functions in Psychosomatic Interrelations." *Psychosom. Med.*, 1:19, 1939 (b).

———: "Brief Psychotherapy in Psychosomatic Problems." *Psychosom. Med.*, 9:98, 1947.

———: *Mid-Century Psychiatry*. Thomas, Springfield, 1953.

Grinker, R. R., and Spiegel, J. P.: *Men Under Stress*. Blakiston, Philadelphia, 1945.

Grinker, R. R., Ham, Geo. C., and Robbins, Fred P.: "Some Psychodynamic Factors in Multiple Sclerosis." *Proceedings Assoc. for Research in Nervous and Mental Diseases*, 28:456, 1950.

Halliday, J. L.: *Psychosocial Medicine: A Study of the Sick Society*. Norton, New York, 1948.

Hartmann, H.: "Comment on the Psychoanalytic Theory of the Ego." *The Psychoanalytic Study of the Child*, 5:74, 1950.

———: "Psychoanalysis and Developmental Psychology." *The Psychoanalytic Study of the Child*, 5:7, 1951.

Henry, J.: "Family Structure and the Transmission of Neurotic Behavior." *Amer. Journ. Orthopsych.*, 21:800, 1951.

———: "Anthropology and Psychosomatics." *Psychosom. Med.*, 11:216, 1949.

Henry, J., and Boggs, J. W.: "Child Rearing, Culture, and the Natural World." *Psychiatry*, 15:261, 1952.

Herold, C. M.: "Critical Analysis of the Elements of Psychic

Functions." *The Psychoanalytic Quarterly,* 10:513, 1941, 11:59, 187, 1942.

Herrick, C. J.: *An Introduction to Neurology.* Saunders, Philadelphia, 1930.

———: *George E. Coghill, Naturalist and Philosopher.* University of Chicago Press, 1949.

Hoffer, W.: "Mouth, Hand and Ego Integration." *The Psychoanalytic Study of the Child,* 3:49, 1949.

———: "Development of the Body Ego." *The Psychoanalytic Study of the Child,* 5:18, 1950.

Holland, H.: *Mental Physiology.* Longmans, Brown, Green, and Longmans, London, 1852.

Hyden, H., and Hartelius, H.: "Stimulation of the Nucleoprotein-Production in the Nerve Cells by Malononitrile and Its Effects on Psychic Functions in Mental Disorders." *Acta Psychiat. et Neurol.,* Suppl. 48, 1948.

Jackson, H.: "A Contribution to the Comparative Study of Convulsions." *Brain,* 9:482, 1886.

Jennings, H. S.: "Behavior of Lower Organisms." *Journ. Exp. Zool.,* 2:473, 1900, Columbia University Press, New York, 1906.

Johnson, A. L.: "The Constitutional Factor in Skull Form and Dental Occlusion." *Amer. Journ. of Orthodontics and Oral Surgery,* 26:627, 1939.

Johnson, C. S.: "The Influence of Social Science on Psychiatry." Chapter XI in Grinker, *Mid-Century Psychiatry.* Thomas, Springfield, 1953.

Katz, D.: *Gestalt Psychology.* Ronald Press, New York, 1950.

Keith, A.: *Human Embryology and Morphology.* Fourth Edition, Longmans, Green and Co., New York, 1921.

Keith, A., and Campion, G.: "A Contribution to the Mechanism of Growth of the Human Face." *The Dental Record*, 42:61, 365, 1922.

Kepecs, J.: "Some Patterns of Displacement of Somatic Symptoms." *Psychosom. Med.* (in press), 1953.

Kepecs, J., Robin, M., and Brunner, M. J.: "Relationship Between Certain Emotional States and Exudation into the Skin." *Psychosom. Med.*, 13:10, 1951.

Klein, M.: *The Psychoanalysis of Children*. Hogarth, London, 1932.

Klüver, H.: "Functional Differences Between the Occipital and Temporal Lobes, with Special Reference to the Interrelation of Behavior and Extracerebral Mechanism." In *Cerebral Mechanisms in Behavior*. John Wiley & Sons, New York, 1951.

Klüver, H., and Bucy, P. B.: "An Analysis of Certain Effects of Bilateral Temporal Lobectomy in the Rhesus Monkey with Special Reference to 'Psychic Blindness.' " *Journ. of Psychol.*, 5:33, 1938.

————: "A Preliminary Analysis of the Functions of the Temporal Lobes in Monkeys." *Transact. Amer. Neurol. Assoc.*, p. 170, 1939, and *Arch. Neurol. & Psych.*, 42:979, 1939, 44:1142, 1940.

Korchin, S., Persky, H., Basowitz, H., and Grinker, R. R.: *An Experimental Investigation in Anxiety: Interdisciplinary Research in Life Situations*, 1953.

Kretschmer, W.: *Medizinische Psychologie*. Fourth Edition, Springer, Berlin, 1930.

Kubie, L. S.: "Instincts and Homeostasis." *Psychosom. Med.*, 10:15, 1948.

————: *The Central Representation of the Symbolic Process in*

Relation to Psychosomatic Disorders. 1953 (to be published) (a).

————: "The Distortion of the Symbolic Process in Neurosis and Psychosis." *Journ. American Psychoanalytic Association,* 1:59, 1953 (b).

Kuntz, A.: *Visceral Innervation and Its Relation to Personality.* Thomas, Springfield, 1951.

Levy, D. M.: "Fingersucking and Accessory Movements in Early Infancy." *Amer. Journ. Psych.,* 7:881, 1928.

————: "Animal Psychology in Its Relation to Psychiatry." Chapter XV in *Dynamic Psychiatry,* edited by Alexander and Ross. University of Chicago Press, 1952.

Lewin, B.: *The Psychoanalysis of Elation.* Norton, New York, 1950.

Lillie, R. S.: *General Biology and Philosophy of Organism.* University of Chicago Press, 1945.

Logan, H. G. Wm.: "A Histologic Study of the Anatomic Structures Forming the Oral Cavity." *J.A.D.A.,* 22:3, 1935.

MacLean, P. D.: "Psychosomatic Disease and the 'Visceral Brain.'" *Psychosom. Med.,* 11:338, 1949.

Manhold, J. H., and Manhold, V. W.: "A Preliminary Report on the Study of the Relationship of Psychosomatics to Oral Conditions." *Science,* 110:585, 1949.

Margolin, S.: "Psychoanalysis and the Dynamics of Psychosomatic Medicine." *Journ. American Psychoanalytic Association,* 1953 (to be published).

Margolin, S. G., Orringer, D., Kaufman, M. R., Winkelstein, A., Hollander, F., Janowitz, H., Stein, A., and Levy, M. H.: "Variations of Gastric Functions during Conscious and Unconscious Conflict States." *Proc. Association for Research in Nervous and Mental Diseases,* 29:656, 1950.

Mead, M.: "The Concept of Culture and the Psychosomatic Approach." *Psychiatry*, 10:57, 1947.

————: *Male and Female*. Wm. Morrow, New York, 1949.

————: "Some Relationships Between Social Anthropology and Psychiatry." Chapter XIII in *Dynamic Psychiatry*, Edited by Alexander and Ross. University of Chicago Press, 1952.

Mead, M., and MacGregor, F. C.: *Growth and Culture. A Photographic Study of Balinese Childhood*. G. P. Putnam's Sons, New York, 1951.

Menninger, K.: *Man Against Himself*. Harcourt, Brace, New York, 1938.

Michaels, J. J.: "Parallel Between Persistent Eneuresis and Delinquency in the Psychosomatic Personality." *Amer. Journ. Orthopsych.*, 11:260, 1941.

————: "A Psychiatric Adventure in Comparative Pathophysiology of the Infant and Adult." *Journ. Nerv. & Ment. Dis.*, 100:49, 1944.

————: "The Concept of Integration in Psychoanalysis." *Journ. Nerv. & Ment. Dis.*, 102:54, 1945.

Mirsky, I. A.: *Psychoanalysis and the Biological Sciences*. 1953. (to be published).

Monakow, C. von: *The Emotions, Morality and the Brain*. New York, 1925.

Morris, C.: *The Open Self*. Prentice-Hall, New York, 1948.

Murphy, G.: *Personality. A Biosocial Approach to Origins and Structure*. Harper & Bros., New York, 1947.

Papez, J. W.: "A Proposed Mechanism of Emotion." *Arch. Neurol. & Psych.*, 38:725, 1937.

Parsons, T.: *Toward a General Theory of Action*. Harvard University Press, 1951 (a).

————: "Illness and the Role of the Physician. A Sociological

Perspective." *Amer. Journ. Orthopsych.*, 21:452, 1951 (b).

————: *Psychoanalysis and Social Science with Special Reference to the Oedipus Problem.* 1953 (to be published).

Pavlov, I. P.: *Conditioned Reflexes.* International Publishing Co., New York, 1928.

Pendelton, E. C.: "Anatomy of the Face and Mouth from the Standpoint of the Denture Prosthetist." *J.A.D.A.*, 33:219, 1946.

Penfield, W., and Erikson, K.: *Epileptic Seizure Patterns.* Thomas, Springfield, 1951.

Persky, H., Grinker, R. R., and Mirsky, I. A.: "The Excretion of Hippuric Acid in Subjects with Free Anxiety." *Journ. Clin. Invest.*, 29:110, 1950 (a).

Persky, H., Grinker, R. R., Mirsky, I. A., and Gamm, S.: "Life Situations, Emotions and the Excretion of Hippuric Acid in Anxiety States." *Proc. Association for Research in Nervous and Mental Diseases*, 29:297, 1950 (b).

Persky, H., Gamm, S., and Grinker, R. R.: "Correlation Between Fluctuation of Free Anxiety and the Quantity of Hippuric Acid Excretion." *Psychosom. Med.*, 14:34, 1952.

Piaget, J.: *Child's Conception of Physical Causality.* Harcourt, Brace, New York, 1930.

Piers, G., and Singer, M. B.: *Shame and Guilt.* Thomas, Springfield, 1953.

Rable, C.: *Die Entwicklung des Gesichtes.* Engelmann, Leipzig, 1902.

Rank, B., Putnam, N. C., and Rachlin, G.: "The Significance of the 'Emotional Climate' in Early Feeding Difficulties." *Psychosom. Med.*, 10:279, 1948.

Rapaport, D.: "The Conceptual Model of Psychoanalysis." *Journ. Personality*, 20:56, 1951.

Rapaport, D.: *On the Psychoanalytic Theory of Affects*. (Privately mimeographed, 1952.)

Ruesch, J.: "The Infantile Personality—the Core Problem of Psychosomatic Medicine." *Psychosom. Med.*, 10:134, 1948.

Ruesch, J., and Bateson, G.: *Communication, The Social Matrix of Psychiatry*. Norton, New York, 1951.

Ryle, J. A.: "The Visceral Neuroses." *Lancet*, 2:297, 353, 407, 1939.

Saul, L. J.: "The Physiological Effects of Psychoanalytic Therapy." *Proc. Association for Research in Nervous and Mental Diseases*, 19:305, Williams & Wilkins, Baltimore, 1939.

Schneider, D. E.: *The Growth Concept of Nervous Integration*. Nerv. & Ment. Dis. Pub. Co., New York, 1949.

Schuntermann, C. E.: "Absorption Ability of the Mucosa of the Mouth." *Zeitschr. f.d. ges. exper. Med.*, 87:259, 1933.

Scott, W. C. M.: "The 'Body Scheme' in Psychotherapy." *British Journ. Med. Psychol.*, 22:139, 1949.

Selye, H.: "The General Adaptation Syndrome and the Diseases of Adaptation." *Journ. Clin. Endocrinology*, 6:117, 1946.

Sheldon, Wm. H.: The Varieties of Human Physique. Harper and Brothers, New York, 1940.

Sherrington, C.: *Man on His Nature*. Macmillan, New York, 1941.

Sperling, M.: "The Role of the Mother in Psychosomatic Disorders in Childhood." *Psychosom. Med.*, 11:377, 1949.

Spiegel, J. P.: *Transactional Foci within a Total Field as Determinants of Human Behavior*. 1953 (to be published).

Spitz, R. A.: "Anaclitic Depression: An Inquiry into the Genesis of Psychiatric Conditions in Early Childhood." *The Psychoanalytic Study of the Child*, 2:313, 1947.

Spitz, R. A.: "Relevancy of Direct Infant Observation." *The Psychoanalytic Study of the Child,* 5:66, 1950.

Stanton, A. H., and Schwartz, M. S.: "Observations on Dissociation as Social Participation." *Psychiatry,* 12:330, 1949.

———: "Relevancy of Direct Infant Observation." *Psychiatry,* 5:66, 1950.

Stainbrook, E.: "Psychosomatic Medicine in the Nineteenth Century." *Journ. Psychosom. Med.,* 14:211, 1952.

Stone, L.: "Concerning the Psychogenesis of Somatic Disease." *International Journ. Psychoanal.,* 19:63, 1938.

Szasz, T. S.: "Psychoanalysis and the Autonomic Nervous System." *Psychoanalytic Review,* 39:115, 1952.

Thetford, W. N.: "Fantasy Perceptions in the Personality Development of Normal and Deviant Children." *American Journ. Orthopsych.,* 22:542, 1952.

Thompson, L.: "Personality and Government." *America Indigena,* 11:235, 1951.

———: "Contributions to the Analysis and Synthesis of Knowledge." *Proc. Amer. Acad. Arts and Sciences,* 80:173, 1952.

Tolman, E. C.: *Collected Papers in Psychology.* University of California Press, Berkeley, 1951.

Toman, J. E. P., and Taylor, J. D.: "Mechanisms of Action and Metabolism of Anticonvulsants." *Epilepsia,* III ser. 1:31, 1952.

Williams, P. N.: "Determining the Shape of the Normal Arch." *Dental Cosmos,* 59:596, 1917.

Whyte, L. L.: *The Next Development in Man.* Henry Holt, New York, 1948.

Wolff, H. G.: "Life Stress and Bodily Disease—A Formulation." *Proc. Association for Research in Nervous and Mental Diseases,* 29:1059, 1950.

Selected References from the Recent Psychosomatic Literature

1. Engel, George L.: Studies of ulcerative colitis I. Clinical data bearing on the nature of the somatic process. *Psychosom. Med., 16,* 496, 1954. Studies of ulcerative colitis II. The nature of the somatic processes and the adequacy of psychosomatic hypotheses. *Amer. J. Med., 16,* 416, 1954. Studies of ulcerative colitis III. The nature of the psychologic processes. *Amer. J. Med., 19,* 231, 1955.
2. Magoun, Horace W.: *The Waking Brain.* Charles C. Thomas: Springfield, Illinois, 1958.
3. Mason, John: Visceral functions of the nervous system. *Ann. Rev. Physiol., 21,* 353, 1959.
4. Mirsky, I. Arthur: The psychosomatic approach to the etiology of clinical disorders. *Psychosom. Med., 19,* 424, 1957.
5. Tinbergen, N.: *The Study of Instinct.* Oxford University Press: Oxford, England 1951.
6. Lorenz, K.: *King Solomon's Ring.* Methuen: London, England 1952.

7. Harlow, Harry S. and Zimmerman, Robert R.: Affectional responses in the infant monkey. *Science, 130*, 421, August 21, 1958.

8. Bowlby, John: The nature of the child's tie to his mother. *Internat. J. Psychoanal., 39*, 350, 1958.

9. Richmond, Julius B. and Lipton, Earle: Some aspects of the neurophysiology of the new-born and their implications for child development. Page 78 in Jessner, Lucy and Pavenstedt, Eleanor: *Dynamic Psychopathology in Childhood*. Grune and Stratton: New York, 1959.

10. Engel, George L. and Reichsman, Franz: A study of an infant with a gastric fistula I. Behavior and the rate of total hydrochloric acid secretion. *Psychosom. Med., 18*, 374, 1956.
    Engel, George L. and Reichsman, Franz: Spontaneous and experimentally induced depressions in an infant with a gastric fistula; a contribution to the problem of depression. *J. Amer. Psychoanal. Assoc., 4*, 428, 1956.

11. Lacey, John I.: The evaluation of autonomic responses: Toward a general solution. *Ann. N. Y. Acad. Sci., 67*, 123, 1956.

12. Lilly, John C.: Mental effects of reduction of ordinary levels of physical stimuli on intact, healthy person. *Psychiat. Research Report No. 5, Amer. Psychiat. Assoc.*, page 1, 1956.

13. Bexton, W. H., Heron, W., and Scott, T. H.: Effects of decreased variation in the sensory environment. *Canad. J. Psychol., 8,* 70, 1954.

14. Wexler, Donald, Mendelson, Jack, Leiderman, Herbert, and Solomon, Philip: Sensory deprivation: A technique for studying psychiatric aspects of stress. *A.M.A. Arch. Neurol. Psychiat., 79,* 225, 1958.

15. Mendelson, Jack, Kubzansky, P., Leiderman, P. H., Wexler, D., DuToit, C., and Solomon, P.: Catechol amine excretion and behavior during sensory deprivation. *A.M.A. Arch. gen. Psychiat., 2,* 147, 1960.

16. Hinkle, Lawrence E. and Wolff, Harold: The nature of man's adaptation to his total environment and the relation of this to illness. *A.M.A. Arch. Int. Med., 99,* 442, 1957.
    Hinkle, Lawrence E., Christenson, William H., Kane, Francis D., Ostfeld, Adrian, Thetford, William N., and Wolff, Harold G.: An investigation of the relation between life experience, personality characteristics, and general susceptibility to illness. *Psychosom. Med., 20,* 278, 1958.
    Hinkle, Lawrence E., Kane, Francis D., Christenson, William N., and Wolff, Harold G.: Hungarian refugees: Life experiences and features influencing participation in the revolution and subsequent flight. *Amer. J. Psychiat., 116,* 16, 1959.

17. Ruesch, Jurgen and Kees, Weldon: *Non-verbal Communication. Notes on the Visual Perception of Human Relations.* University of California Press: Berkeley and Los Angeles, California, 1956.
Ruesch, J.: *Disturbed Communications.* W. W. Norton and Company: New York, 1957.

18. Fisher, S. and Cleveland, S. E.: *Body Image and Personality.* Van Nostrand: Princeton, New Jersey, 1958.

19. Engel, George L.: A Unified Concept of Health and Disease. *Perspectives in Biology and Medicine, 3,* 459, 1960.

20. Engel, George L.: Selection of clinical material in psychosomatic medicine. The need for a new physiology. *Psychosom. Med., 16,* 368, 1954.

21. Schmale, Arthur H., Jr.: Relationship of separation and depression to disease. I. A report on a hospitalized medical population. *Psychosom. Med., 20,* 259, 1958.

Index

Index

hippuric acid, 171–173
Hoffer, W., 121
Holland, Henry, 12, 20, 25, 39
hormonal secretions, 144
hostility, oral, 105
humors, influence of, 21
Hyden, H., 22

id, 51, 63, 76, 122, 150–151
identification, 133–134
Ilg, F. L., 83
illness, effect of on infant, 92, 93
impressions, effect of early, 96–100
"in-between," area of, 90, 95, 102
individual differences, causes of, 91–92
infant, 122, 156
  compared with depressed person, 110, 137
  discovery of finger or hand, 121
  expression of, 110
  hereditary functional patterns of, 70
  illness, effect of, 92, 93
  influence of culture on, 95
  malnutrition of, 107
  mouth functions in, 105, 119–120
  needs of, 128–131
  orality in, 117
  reactions of, 61–63, 71–72, 86, 123
  reality for, 130–131
  rushing the development of, 93
instincts, 73, 88, 99–100, 150, 156
Institute for Psychosomatic Research and Training of the Michael Reese Hospital, 10
insulin coma, behavior in, 115
integration, 78, 142–165, 167
integrative capacity of child, 132–133
intrapersonal functions, 166–170
irritability, 148, 176–177
Ittelson, W. H., 155

Jackson, Hughlings, 78, 80
Jennings, H. S., 20
Johnson, Charles, 51

Katz, D., 109
Keith, A., 107
kennetic inquiry, 153
Kepecs, J., 66, 67
Klein, Melanie, 123, 130
Klüver, H., 114, 115, 124

Korchin, S., 174
Kretschmer, W., 24
Kubie, L. S., 79, 88–89, 178
Kuntz, A., 79

learning, 72, 73, 102, 130–131
Levy, David, 23, 120
Lewin, B., 124, 125, 130
libido, 178
libido theory, see Freud, Sigmund
Liddell, H. S., 23
life and death instincts, 42
"Life Situations, Emotions and Bodily Change," Wolff, 44
Lillie, R. S., 146
lobectomy, 114–117, 124
Logan, H. G. William, 111
Lombroso, C., 108

MacGregor, F. C., 49
MacLean, P. D., 79, 178
malnutrition, effect of, 107
Manhold, J. H., 111
Manhold, V. W., 111
Manual of Child Psychology, Carmichael, 90
Margolin, S., 57, 86–88
maturation, 86, 134
Mead, M., 49, 84
melancholia, 121
melancholic, expression of, 110
memory patterns, 155
Menninger, Karl, 27
mental diseases, bodily cause of, 21
mentation, 73–74
Michaels, J. J., 78
mind-body problem in ancient medicine, 20–21
Mirsky, I. A., 62, 90–91
Monakow, C. von, 21
monkeys, temporal lobectomy of, 114–117, 124
Morris, C., 25
mother, dependence on, 88
mother-child relationship, 50, 74, 85, 89, 91–95, 99, 103, 126, 129–131, 133, 136, 140
  during feeding, 120–121
  observation of, 83–84, 125
  recent changes in, 49
mouth, 105–117